Changing the Odds

An entrepreneur's guide to success

Richard Bostock

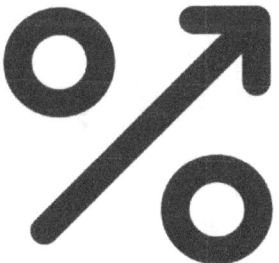

First published in the United Kingdom in 2021 by
Changing Odds Ltd

www.changing-odds.com

Copyright © Richard Bostock 2021

The moral right of the author has been asserted.

All rights reserved. Without limiting the rights under copyright reserved above, no part of this publication may be reproduced, stored or introduced into a retrieval system, or transmitted, in any form or by means (electronic, mechanical, photocopying, recording or otherwise), without the prior written permission of both the copyright owner and the publisher of the book.

ISBN 9781739757021

For Rupert, Herbie and Gary

The Future

Contents

Chapter 1 - Introduction 1
Chapter 2 - Basic Principles 9
Chapter 3 - The Essentials 13
Chapter 4 - Customers and markets 25
Chapter 5 - Finance Essentials 48
Chapter 6 - Funding 66
Chapter 7 - Making the business work 85
Chapter 8 - Developing a strategy 96
Chapter 9 - Avoiding failure – or understanding how to deal with it. 117
Chapter 10 - The Future 131
Chapter 11 - Success and the alternatives… 140
Chapter 12 - Types of Entrepreneur – and possible implications 157
Chapter 13 - The Intrapreneur 177
Chapter 14 - Distilling the Process 192
Appendix 1 199
Notes for each chapter 211
Acknowledgements 222

Preface

This book is based on over 35 years of direct experience in helping entrepreneurs build successful business and also witnessing failures.

The author, Richard Bostock has worked on major turnrounds of established businesses, restructured many more and has shared many of these experiences as an MBA strategy tutor, trainer, mentor and advisor in many industries.

The book is full of real life examples which bring the ideas and theories to life and demonstrate the skill of distilling complex problems into manageable components without over-simplifying the critical elements.

The final chapter in the book demonstrates this in a distillation of the entire book into a series of steps that should be followed in every start.

The book is supported by a website which provides further insights and ideas along with access to the templates and models used in the book.

www.changing-odds.com

Chapter 1 - Introduction

This book is about failure. It highlights the futility of starting your own business and of becoming a successful entrepreneur.

Sounds negative – look at the statistics:
Start ups and business "death rates"
Failures within the first 12 months – around 20%
Failures within 3 years – around 60%
There are plenty of estimates but these estimates reflect some of the realities.

The alleged reasons for failure are well publicised and written about:

- Under- capitalised
- Poor marketing
- Under-estimating competition
- Poor management

Fix these four basics and you have a successful business? Wrong. There's more going on than just these four simplistic statements. The first clue is that the statements are vague and non-specific and should be prompting questions such as:

- How much capital do I need?
- What is marketing and how can I use it effectively?
- What is my competition and HOW am I going to compete?
- Just what management skills do I need, do I have them, can I get them?

These questions start you on a path that might lead to success but the real success comes from how curious you are and how you use the curiosity to build your business ideas.

There are no easy answers and no perfect answers. We live in uncertain times – but this was ever the case for those living in any era. The one thing we can guarantee is change. Some things may be predictable – but if that's the case everyone knows, so we just know the same as everyone else.

This highlights a key attribute of a successful entrepreneur – the ability to think differently, to see different patterns in the predictable data, to envisage different futures.

One of the reasons for high business failure rates is the idea that because I'm good at something – a trade, a profession, a particular skill – I can build a successful business around it.

If this was true every carpenter, plumber, web designer, lawyer, dentist would be successful if they set up a business rather than working for someone else. This is clearly not the case so something else must be going on.

Many people start in business as a sole trader or small partnership. It's quick and easy with very few rules and restrictions (more on this is Chapter 2). They might have left an employer and see the opportunity of earning more and "being your own boss". The problem is they join a vast group of self-employed who are all just as skilled with similar training and experience – or they might be better. How do you survive – let alone grow and prosper? It's simple, your skill and expertise are just resources which can be traded if you can find the customers. Until you find the customers you have to buy the tools and materials you need, you have to pay the rent, eat – and perhaps support a family.

Suddenly the list of four things you need to succeed come into focus:

- The need for capital
- The need to find customers – marketing
- The need to survive the many competitors out there
- The need to manage more than just the job – be that installing a boiler, filling a tooth, designing a web page or launching a challenge to Facebook

This explains why many self-employed struggle and even the successful ones realise that time on the job (earning money) is limited by all the "non-productive" time. Suddenly the earnings premium disappears and time working increases and increases. It only needs one job to go wrong, a client to refuse to pay, a supplier to let you down on a crucial piece of equipment. These are all the joys of being your own boss.

But what if you have bigger ideas – starting a larger business venture and even becoming a "unicorn" company? A Unicorn is a company that achieves a $1 billion valuation during the startup phase. It's important to recognize that this valuation usually comes before the business has generated any profits or even started making substantial sales.

Or what if you want to use your business to help people and improve communities and society – a social enterprise?

The same principles apply, you just have to flex and adjust and use the right tools for the job.

This book is about helping you work out what type of business you want to start and then providing you with the range of tools which you will need. It helps you choose the right tools for the job in hand. The objective is to be practical and realistic, however there are some useful academic theories and frameworks that can help – we'll use these as necessary but only where they can add value.

I'm trying to help you Change the Odds and succeed.

So why bother? Can it be made better?

Of course it can – there are many successful businesses out there, growing and prospering.

So where do we start to make it a successful start-up?

The first and most important issue is to recognise that an entrepreneur must wear different hats – and be comfortable in them. This requires thinking beyond the technical job. Lots of people are qualified to fill a tooth or to fit a boiler – why would they pick you?

In the old days we had the printed version of Yellow Pages. Many viewed this as an essential part of marketing/advertising. The problem is the sheer scale and size of the publication. There are hundreds and thousands of businesses offering the same service – how do you stand out so that a customer picks you. This explains the volume of businesses called AAA or aardvark – it just puts them at the front of the section.

Nowadays we have social media – Facebook, LinkedIn, Twitter, Instagram etc. This gives the opportunity for electronic word of mouth, but there's still lots of people out there competing for the customer's attention. There's lots of noise and distractions.

The entrepreneur needs to think beyond this basic communication process and consider how to differentiate the business and even create magnets that draw customers and business. Suddenly the technical skills and expertise are simply resources that have little value unless they can be combined with other resources to create something special. It may still be a dentist business or a plumbing business but it has an edge. If this edge is good enough it can mean that customer demand will outstrip the resources of the founder/entrepreneur – then you have a growth model and you employ people to do the technical stuff so that you spend more and more time growing the business – doing the real entrepreneur stuff.

Many entrepreneurs describe their experiences as being on a roller coaster ride. This is true to a certain extent with a few exceptions – you're not in control of a real roller coaster, you just sit on it. The ride finishes at some stage and you can get off and get your breath and heart rate back under control. Neither of these scenarios fit the real entrepreneur experience.

That's the basic platform so let's get started and change the odds.

The Structure of the Book

There are 14 chapters and each chapter stands on its own so there are often overlaps with other chapters. This is quite deliberate and helps to reinforce some of the important issues.

How you read the book is up to you. You may even go straight to Chapter 14 and read how the content of the book distils into a plan of action and then work back through relevant chapters.

The later chapters help in developing a strategic mindset and the curiosity and critical reflection which drives every successful entrepreneur – regardless of background.

Chapters 1 to 3 looks at the different starting points:

Who are we and what do we want to do?

The different structures and formats that are appropriate.

The overarching issues facing each approach.

Creating a framework for developing each type of business.

Chapters 4 to 7 considers each approach in some detail and provides a framework for applying various tools and frameworks which leads to the critical assessment of the viability of your idea.

Chapters 8 to 13 develops the ideas building an effective strategy for the business and the thinking processes that can drive success and avoid (or reduce the risk of) failure. For each type of business and how to use a business plan for your own focus as well as generating funding, dealing with suppliers, customers and competitors. This develops into the risks and opportunities of growth and sustainability and how to build effective strategies that go beyond vague aspirations.

You will notice that at the beginning of each chapter and some sections there is a question. Some of the skills of a successful entrepreneur that you will discover as you work through this book involve being curious, keeping an open mind and reflecting on what you have done and where it might be improved. One of the ways to develop these skills is to start each stage of learning by checking what you think you know and if you have any entrenched beliefs which might impact on your thinking and decision making.

I would like you to consider each question before you read the chapter and try to write down your answers and ideas. You may consider the question is irrelevant or even stupid. That's fine – write down what you think. When you've finished the chapter go back to your notes and write down any new feelings, ideas and reflections.

This type of writing and reflection is a powerful learning tool and it helps to develop an open mind to new thoughts, information, evidence. If you haven't changed your ideas by reading the chapter that is fine – you've just reinforced some good ideas. If you've changed your ideas, you've just learned some new skills which should help you as an entrepreneur.

You can, of course, just make the decision to ignore the questions and just read the book. Even in this situation try to take a little time to reflect on each piece of information, evidence and technique and see how it fits with your current thinking and knowledge.

I think you may be surprised at the results.

The book also uses insights, quotes and material from other authors, academics and practitioners to reinforce and expand some of the ideas. The first insight comes from an excellent book by Eric Ries – The Lean Startup – that uses his own experiences as an entrepreneur to challenge some of the outdated and conventional thinking about entrepreneurs. This is in the Introduction to The Lean Startup[1]:

"I have learned from both my own successes and failures and those of many others that it's the boring stuff that matters the most. Startup success is not a consequence of good genes or being in the right place at the right time. Startup success can be engineered by following the right process, which means it can be learned, which means it can be taught."

I fully agree with this statement and it fits with my own experiences and observations.

The book is intended to help this learning process.

And finally, the Chapter 14 distils all the issues covered in the book to provide a framework for moving from initial idea to a successful business – and answers the question as to when to write a business plan and what should it contain.

Enjoy!

"In time of drastic change, it is the learners who inherit the future. Those who have finished learning find themselves equipped to live in a world that no longer exists." Eric Hoffer

Chapter 2 - Basic Principles

Warm up Question:
What is your ultimate purpose in setting up a business? What structure do you think best suits this purpose?

The way you set up the business can be quite critical. The structure can limit some opportunities or help you exploit other opportunities. However, much depends on your purpose.

Although sole trader and partnerships form the majority of businesses (in the UK) the most common format for a business which intends to grow is a limited liability company as this provides a good platform for developing a sustainable business, building a brand and raising finance to fund growth. If you are planning a small, lifestyle business which you don't want to grow then there are simpler structures. Appendix 1 summarises the common formats available in many countries – but check local rules and regulations.

The range of legal and regulatory frameworks is quite broad from country to country and it is important that anyone planning to start a business checks out the rules where they plan to operate. In some places the rules can be quite complicated and may require the advice of legal and financial/accountancy experts in local rules.

This highlights an important principle before you even get started – find out for yourself and then use the experts to reinforce and support your knowledge and understanding. Never rely on "outsiders" to make decisions for you or take control of critical aspects of the business. Use the experts as resources to underpin and reinforce your own ideas.

The structure of the business can influence many factors, in particular the opportunities and risks and limitations in raising finance. These factors are often reflected in the legislation and regulations which are usually designed and implemented to encourage business while also looking after the interests of key stakeholders.

Governments want to encourage employment and activities that stimulate economic measures such as GDP and disposable income. All these factors have a big by-product – taxation which can be applied in a range of ways including:

- Tax on corporate profits
- Taxation on individual earnings
- Social taxes that reflect a tax on employment (eg National Insurance in the UK)
- Value added tax on purchases
- Tax on capital gains and inheritance

Some of these have an immediate impact such as employment taxes, others have a longer term impact such as tax on corporate profits and VAT, while capital gains and inheritance tax are long term issues that impact if/when the founder exits the business.

All of these factors also impact on investors in the business. Investing is a business in itself.

It's also important to recognise that taxation underpins the legislation for running businesses in every country. Taxation might be driven by economic considerations but it is ultimately a political decision so that it is always subject to change – you need to keep your options under review.

All of these issues need to be considered from the outset – whether you are planning to run a simple, one person business or want to become a "unicorn" (a start-up with an early valuation in excess of $1 billion), or anything in between.

Chapter 3 - The Essentials

Warm up Question:
What do you think are the essentials for any entrepreneur when starting a business?

Over the years I've evaluated many business plans and early stage ideas. I've sat on a variety of panels evaluating business ideas for various purposes – funding, visa applications etc.
There is one common feature that separates the good ones from the less good or downright bad.
Remember in the Introduction I highlighted why businesses fail and the two key issues are understanding your market and your competitors. The reality is that everything interconnects – if you don't know the market and/or under estimate the competition your business will take longer to become established and reach break even and profitability. This means your estimates of capital requirements is too low, you then run out of cash and the inevitable happens.
Typical discussions I've had with start-ups:
Q - What is your target market?
A - Everyone with a home.

Q - Where are you sourcing your product/raw material?
A - China
Q - Why?
A - Isn't that where everyone gets things from as it's cheap…….

Q - Who are your competitors?
A - I don't have any because my business is unique

These responses may seem nonsense – but they actually happen. The responses show a lack of understanding about the fundamentals of business.

- You need to be curious.
- You need to be challenging.
- You need to question your own thinking.
- You need to be wary of 'group think' where everyone reinforces popular ideas – that may just be myths.

To overcome this you need some hard work doing research. Not just a simple generic Google search but some in-depth research that joins up the different elements of your business idea and starts to test and evaluate its feasibility.

A good starting point is to take your product/service idea and define your perfect customer. Why would they buy from you? What level of price might they pay? What expectations do they have and how will you meet and even exceed them?

Outcomes of research:

Realistic assessment of market size and potential sales

Understanding segmentation issues (specific target groups)

Understanding what to avoid - lack of research and we accept anything regardless of the sense

What do you need to research?

Everything that is relevant. This is where a good mentor can be invaluable – just asking the question "have you thought of……"? can open up whole areas of relevant research.

There are some fundamental basics that you can pick up from many marketing and strategy courses which are covered in more detail in Chapter 8 on Strategy. Here's an overview and you can find more details of the academic stuff in the bibliography section.

Just making a start is often a big hurdle so start with something easy that's relevant:

You

Who are you, what can you do, what are your skills and experiences?

What do you enjoy? What do you hate?

This is not a conventional CV but a personal profile that covers everything. Most people are surprised when they do this. Don't do it all at once – take some time, even a few weeks. Keep a notepad or device to jot down notes and thoughts.

Being wedded to an idea for too long.

I'm always cautious about putting this forward as a problem. A good entrepreneur has a vision of some future state – perhaps a new product or service or a different way of doing something. There are always barriers and obstacles so the entrepreneur needs to be tenacious, persistent and sometimes just plain obstinate.

However, this can be a major problem if the idea is not based on solid research, evaluation of the evidence, diagnosis of the key issues and a realistic plan of action. Yes, there might be some luck involved, timing may be critical but the risks are understood as far as is possible,

If the evidence and diagnosis doesn't support the idea then a good entrepreneur will walk away and look elsewhere. There is often a positive outcome. As well as not losing a lot of time and money pursuing an unrealistic business, the accumulated knowledge and understanding of markets, competitors, supply chains etc will often open a new door which leads to success.

This highlights an important point about success. A successful business is less about what you do than how you do it and underpinning this is why you're doing it and why it's relevant.

I always recommend budding entrepreneurs to watch the Simon Sinek video "Start with why"[1].

https://www.ted.com/talks/simon_sinek_how_great_leaders_inspire_action?language=en

This is why so many business plans are bad, boring and fail to excite – they usually start with "what" is being done and then progress to the technical analysis of how it's done and completely miss the vital element of "Why?".

If you can find a way of communicating the "Why" then you start to instill curiosity in the people you're talking to – rather than indifference and even boredom.

The reaction you want is to get the audience to say "That's really interesting, so *how* do you do it….?" They are now hooked and importantly they feel more in control of the discussion – even though they are actually building on your agenda.

Why is this important? Even with an innovative new product or service the "what" is uninspiring – as highlighted by Sinek. Think about when someone has made a pitch to you and they have started with "What". All you are thinking is "Why is this relevant to me?"

Let's be clear the "how" and the "what" are still important but not at the start. Another important point is to keep the "Why" as brief as possible. You are communicating a feeling or idea – not getting into a long monologue about what motivates you. Ten seconds may be enough for the "Why". More than sixty seconds is likely to be too detailed.

Some may call this an "elevator" pitch but the "Why" is just a part of an elevator pitch – but absolutely essential.

Starting with "Why" provides a platform for differentiating you and your business from competitors. Even if you are unique you still have to convince your potential customer to commit to your product or service. If it's new they will see this as a risk and this creates a potential barrier to the sales process. We consider some of the ways of overcoming these fears in Chapter 4.

The Paradox of Unicorns

A Unicorn is a start-up business that achieves a valuation of a billion dollars at an early stage. They are often technology based and usually have a product or service that disrupts existing markets or industries. The valuation comes from being able to attract substantial early-stage funding from investors, venture capital and private equity firms. An important characteristic is the requirement to Get Big Fast – often supported by first mover advantage.

The thinking is that building scale quickly gets unit costs down and discourages competition.

Unfortunately, there's a lot more to building a successful business than scale and unit cost projections.

How to lose $1.2 billion in a short space of time

Part of this book is about avoiding failure. There are examples of businesses that stood no chance of succeeding but still managed to raise and spend vast amounts of money. Most people have not heard of Webvan[2]. It was an early "disruptor" to grocery retailing introducing an online grocery service in 1999.

It took its first order in June 1999 and when it went bust in June 2001 it had burnt around $1.2 billion of investors' money.

Despite all the hype about a new business model that changed the economics of online businesses it simply ignored many of the established basics for any business. The investors also ignored the same basics. A few facts:

The founders and senior executive staff had no prior experience in the retail grocery business. They were a tech start-up so their entire focus was on the technology – they just happened to be selling groceries. This meant they didn't understand a basic fact about the grocery sales – it has one of the lowest profit margins of any business - between 1% and 2% of sales.

Another simple fact – groceries have a short shelf life. If you don't sell in the right quantities in relation to stock levels you get lots of wastage which shrinks your profits – which are already small.

It's estimated the company needed an average order size of $103. In February 2000, the average order was $80. By the end of that year, it had increased to only $81.

In 2000, the company's daily expenses averaged $1.8 million. Daily sales averaged $489,000.

The company just never got to break even (see Chapter 5)

All of this is bad enough but they compounded the problems by investing vast amounts in specialist warehouses or distribution centres with computerised conveyors, order picking systems etc. Don't forget the founders were technology based.

Just a month after taking the first order it started a project to build 26 distribution centres across the US within 2 years. Webvan paid a billion dollars for the distribution centers.

Each center was 350,000 square feet and fully automated with over 4 miles of conveyor belts in each.

Each center only operated at 35% of its capacity.

Webvan launched an IPO in the early stages and at it's peak the company was valued at over $7 billion.

There's lots more detail that could be added but be aware that Unicorns are not always what they seem and you ignore the fundamentals at your peril.

Any business whether it's a sole trader or an aspiring Unicorn must not ignore the basic fundamentals of a sustainable business model. Remember what I said in the Introduction:

The alleged reasons for failure are well publicised and written about:

Under- capitalised

Poor marketing

Under-estimating competition

Poor management

Fix these four basics and you have a successful business? Wrong. There's more going on than just these four simplistic statements. The first clue is that the statements are vague and non-specific and should be prompting questions such as:

How much capital do I need?

What is marketing and how can I use it effectively?

What is my competition and HOW am I going to compete?

Just what management skills do I need, do I have them, can I get them?

Webvan had lots of capital but not enough for their business model. They didn't understand the market or industry and assumed a new technology would disrupt the market without understanding the complex connections between the various elements in their business model. They didn't understand the competition and they had the wrong management skills.

Let's imagine an alternative scenario for Webvan:
Their skills are in software development and supply chain logistics – not groceries.

The grocery market is highly competitive with large volumes but very slim profit margins and a lot of major players as well as smaller independent operators.

There is a great need for efficiencies at all stages of the supply chain to minimise waste and maximise customer service.

There is an enormous existing grocery distribution network but with the focus on sales through supermarkets – at the time customers preferred to see and handle what they purchased with a high level of impulse purchases based on this physical interaction. We've all done it – popped out for a bottle of milk but couldn't resist the bag of cookies.

What if Webvan had developed their online grocery business by utilising existing distribution centres and delivery vehicles and used their software expertise to provide customers with a great home delivery service and improved the efficiency of the logistics?

Other companies have built slowly such as Peapod[3] in the US, Tesco[4] in the UK etc and many experienced grocers have struggled to develop effective home delivery.

Don't forget Amazon[5] that had also started only a few years earlier with a dream and vision of technology driving retail sales. The early choices were critical to their eventual success and surviving the dotcom crash of 2000.

Jeff Bezos didn't start Amazon in Seattle for a West Coast lifestyle.

They started small operating out of a garage in Seattle. Why Seattle? There were tax breaks available, it was home to some major book publishing businesses and Boeing provided a large pool of potentially valuable technical staff.

Why books to start with?

The book retailing industry was very traditional, slow moving and quite stable. This made it a good target for disruption.

Books are a simple product – small and easily packaged with easy "recycling" (return to stock) if returned. This compares with online clothing retailers. Existing distribution services (the Postal Service) were a simple and cost effective way to deliver the small parcels. Using the Postal Service avoided the need for building an expensive distribution system.

Products can be easily classified and presented on a website.

Finally, the pricing and working capital model provided the key to the disruption. The cost efficiencies of not holding stock (in the early days) enabled Amazon to undercut traditional book retailers by around 25%.

The operating cycle of the traditional book retail process compared to Amazon shows the opportunity for disruption. This was the business model that created the excitement among investors. The technology was the supporting mechanism that was validated by the numbers.

In 1997 the Amazon operating cycle started with taking delivery of stock from the publishers with the books sold and paid for within 16-17 days. Amazon then paid the book suppliers in 58 days from the start of the cycle. This meant they had 41 days of the full value of the sales in the bank before payment was made to the supplier.

Compare this to a traditional book retailer:

The book enters inventory at Day 0.

The supplier is paid at Day 90.

The customer buys and pays for the book Day 168

This means the book retailer is financing 78 days of working capital.

The whole package actually started to drive increasing book readership and the launch of Harry Potter[6] just added to the growth.

This is the financial model but there was more:

Ease of access for people who struggled to get to a bookshop.

After the initial stage there was a large range of stock for immediate order and delivery.

Easy to use with simple software, recommendations etc.

I hope by now you're starting to see some of the challenges but also the excitement of being an entrepreneur.

The Chapter 5 looks at the Financial issues and how to test the financial viability of your ideas.

Now it's an opportunity to reflect on your ideas around the Introductory Question at the start of the Chapter.

Have your ideas changed and what are the key issues to build into your start-up ideas?

"Experience is great as long as the future resembles the past. If not experience can become downright dangerous."
G Hamel

Chapter 4 - Customers and markets

Warm up Question:
Who are your customers and why are you targeting them? Where are they spending their money now?

You have a great idea for a product, a service, a process, an artistic project, an app......

Your idea has come from some experience or insight. This is usually a highly personal view or vision about the world around you. This flows from many sources – work experience, education background, personal experiences dealing with existing products and services.

These can often be categorised as:

- A perceived "gap" in the market
- Potential for a disruptive business model which changes the customer experience
- Opportunities for a new technology
- Exploitation of an existing technology in a new, innovative way
- Just wanting to do what you're good at

All of these can help to explain why there are challenger banks taking on the established main stream banks. Why there are a multitude of apps providing access to services and products by eliminating large elements of the search process.

Just think about the big successes that fit the profile:
Dyson
Facebook
Google
Amazon

There is a lot of buzz about the new "structure" of platform businesses. These don't actually do anything in the traditional sense but supply a service or platform for trading, information exchange, linking suppliers with customers etc.

I'm old fashioned and just consider that these "new business models" are simply re-engineering the issues highlighted above – they provide a service often using established but developing technology and promote using social media. Many of these businesses require such high volumes of sales that it's hard to see how they will ever become profitable – some never do and fail. The ones listed above have successfully taken a new idea and developed scale – on a global basis. Many fail to get to this scale and crash or just fade away. There's a book by Jonathan Knee – The Platform Delusion[1] – which provides some interesting insights into the realities of the "new business models" and some of the fallacies and myths surrounding platform businesses.

This chapter focuses on understanding markets and customers while acknowledging the opportunities for innovative and creative thinking in the way the business operates. At the end of the chapter, I provide some links to useful resources. It is not intended to be a fast-track MBA in marketing. I focus on the basic principles and the practical issues around taking a good idea to market – and selling it at a price that makes a profit and understanding the timescale for making it work. Without this understanding it becomes very difficult, if not impossible to understand the immediate and long term funding requirements of the business.

To do this you have to consider more than just the marketing. What's the financial structure that you need to support, what are the operational issues that impact on productivity and your ability to scale up and benefit from the economies – the list goes on. But without good marketing supporting the sales process the important people – your target customers – may never know you even exist.

The start of a new business idea is often quite complex:

You have a particular skill that you believe you can exploit better than working for someone else.

You see a gap in the market from personal experience or conversations with people – it may start with "wouldn't it be a good idea if ……..." or "I need X but I can't find anything that suits me".

This is often quite vague to start with and needs some creative thinking as it can become quite complex with the various elements of the business interacting and even competing with one another.

Some simple examples:

Amazon sells books (among other things) and some years ago they announced they would buy back books from customers and re-sell them as second hand. They were criticised by "analysts" (an alternative word for experts) who pronounced this was a big mistake as it would have a negative impact on new book sales (the marketing term is "cannibalise"). However, it was a clever move as it provided a new service to book readers that many of them wanted. It helped to recycle products and even encouraged new book sales because readers created space on their bookshelves – tempting to fill with either new or secondhand books. The customer choice had been extended[2].

At an operational level a book is easy to catalogue, package and deliver. Amazon had to extend it's in house operations but they already had a returns department so this was a relatively simple extension of an existing capability.

Online fashion sales are booming and fast fashion retailers such as Zara[3] (part of the Inditex empire), H&M[4] etc are building their on-line business in response to changing consumer habits.

They have created flexible supply chains with some lines being introduced in only a few weeks rather than bulk purchasing for a whole year which was the original business model.

But don't forget Primark[5] who only have physical stores and don't do online sales. An article in the Economist[6] compares some of the contrasting features between these major fashion businesses. They are notoriously cheap compared with all their competitors and buy in bulk all year round. They had to close all their stores at times due to Covid lockdowns but sales have surged once they re-opened.

Prior to the Covid pandemic Primark Gross Profit % was 41% compared to Inditex at 57% and H&M at 53% - but they all achieved a net profit of around 12%. Why is this relevant? It helps to demonstrate that profitability is linked to understanding the target market and customers and then setting up the business to meet customer needs with a cost structure that helps to maximise profitability.

In the modern world there can be significant levels of service associated with products, and services are often linked to tangible products. Basic examples would include a product which provides extended customer support and maintenance and apps that enable the delivery of a product such as food delivery.

I hope you're beginning to see that the initial idea is just a starting point. While it's important to stay focused on this vision there's a lot of hard work in turning the vision into reality and a viable business. Sometimes this hard work brings a realisation that the original idea is not viable. This is not a failure – it is a sign that you are asking the right questions of yourself and also getting inside the heads of your potential customers.

Indeed, the next iteration of your business thinking will be much stronger. This thinking is always appreciated by customers (they get better products and services) and investors who see depth of thinking, analysis and, importantly, realism.

As you develop your ideas it's important to consider how you build and protect your brand. While patents help to protect your innovative, technical development many businesses rely on products and services where a patent is not feasible or realistic. Indeed, patent protection may be possible but may not be commercially worth while. Patent protection can cost a lot of money – even in the early stages – and costs keep rising. You also have to consider how to protect the patent if it is challenged or infringed. Even with insurance this can become a costly and time consuming process which can distract from the task of running and growing the business.

As far as great invention ideas go, they can come from the most unsuspecting of personalities and do not guarantee immediate commercial viability. Against The Grain author Graham Harris[7], who has utilized over 80 patents and successfully brought to market hundreds of unique print-related products, wrote, "Experts estimate that only one out of every five thousand inventions undergo successful product launches to the extent they result in a good return for their inventor."

According to Harris, successful inventors are those that "form the best habits, to keep them on track and disciplined." One habit Harris mentions is persistence, which helps an inventor to push through barriers and seek out continuous improvements to his own design or an existing one, to make the invention a commercial success. Commitment and dedication are key, but inventors must also take time to develop other crucial skills, including resource management and product design.

This is highlighted in Chapter 8.

The conceptualization of the idea itself – albeit crucial – only makes up a small part of the entire process of getting the product out to market and making it a commercial success. Occasionally, even those with less interesting invention ideas can come up with commercially successful products after diligently following through a rigorous refinement process.

Inventor Isaac Newton once said, "If I have seen further, it is by standing on the shoulders of giants." Many commercially successful inventions, like the radio, the car, the airplane, online survey sites or the iPhone are a combination of technological innovations or an improvement of the existing solution. The famous Thomas Edison, known for inventing the light bulb we know today, actually improved designs and replaced materials from previous electric lighting devices that weren't efficient, didn't last long or were too bright, to the point of commercial viability[8].

Protecting the intellectual property of the business is still important and trade marking your product or service can be critical as well as design protection, copyright and, importantly, trade secrets.

Brand Protection

Before we look at the details it's important to consider the importance of brand and trademarks that help support and protect the brand. At its simplest a brand is just a way to differentiate your product/service from all the other offerings in the marketplace. The internet and global supply chains has made this quite challenging. It's important to check that no one has something similar which may confuse your target customers. Your brand may also be offensive or insulting in another language.

Who wants a car called "prostitute"?

It's no secret that the Spanish word "puta" means prostitute. In 1991 Mazda launched the Laputa minivan. The adds claimed that "Laputa is designed to deliver maximum utility in a minimum space while providing a smooth comfortable ride" and "a lightweight, impact absorbing body".

It was renamed after Latin American dealerships complained.

The key learning issues which are essential:

- Search your proposed company/brand name on the internet.
- Look at different markets.
- Check the name in different languages.
- Check that a logo is readable, memorable and works in different formats(big, small, one colour)
- Does it need a product descriptor to emphasise what it does?

You may need professional help in deciding on the best way of protecting your intellectual property but here are the key features:

Trademarks

Trademarks can be registered or unregistered and are usually linked to a brand with unique characteristics. Trademarks need to be registered in individual countries but there are facilities to register an EU wide and world wide trademark – but this can get expensive and does not always give full protection as each country might not recognize the legitimacy of a trademark.

Check out the local rules and fees.

Designs
Registered designs are often easier than gaining a patent and protection.

Designs must differ from other designs by more than a minor difference and provide distinctive character – somewhat similar to inventiveness, but different test eg:

Whether the 'informed user' would consider the designs to give the same 'overall impression'.

The informed user is not a designer themselves, but a 'clued up' customer. They do their research about what they're buying, so have a pretty good understanding of products in that area

Copyright
Protects the expression of a creative work such as artwork, music, films, books and can include software code – both source code and machine code, GUIs, technical documentation and manuals. It also protects website content, presentations, etc.

It is an automatic right – no need to register anything, but does need to be 'fixed' for protection to start – which means you have to be able to prove the date on which you created the material.

Term of protection varies, but generally is the life of the author + 70 years. It provides protection against copying and is not a monopoly. This often means it is quite difficult to prove and provides limited protection

It's important to keep evidence of ownership & creation date and always mark materials eg Richard Bostock © 2021.

Trade secrets
These help to build and protect your brand. The brand is important as it helps you differentiate your product or service from the competition and aids recognition by customers. The name is supposed to derive from the process of marking cattle and other livestock with a unique sign or brand so that it can be identified and distinguished from other animals to prove ownership.

This might all seem hard work before you've even started trading but you need to consider the long-term viability of the business and going through these processes can help with a fundamental aspect of the research that is necessary to get any business off the ground. It is often called market research and there are many books and courses available on how to go about this. Perhaps the most fundamental aspect of this process is to link your product or service to a potential customer.

Understanding the Customer Persona
My friend and colleague on business start-up boot camps[9] (MMU), Naomi Timperley[10] describes this as understanding the customer persona. Who are they? What are their attitudes and needs? Where are they located?

These are just the starting questions and this takes you well beyond what is often presented in business plans which is an overview of the generic demographics of a particular group of people. This can be useful and interesting but doesn't go far enough in understanding the customer persona. Let me stress this approach covers both business to consumer and business to business situations.

This is one of the most challenging stages in translating the business idea into practical reality. The problem with considering broad demographics in this process is that it ignores the major variations that exist within every demographic area. For example, you may be targeting females between the ages of 16 and 30 for your new online fashion retailing business which provides trendy innovative designs. You might be considering an ethical focus given the increasing criticism of fast fashion linked to labour issues in emerging economies, disposal of unused and unwanted clothes, short life-cycle for the clothes et cetera. These issues will start to determine your manufacturing and supply chain processes which will have an impact on cost which in turn impacts on potential selling prices. This leads us to a more precise and focused business model of a range of products which will have a price point above the budget prices of the major fast fashion businesses.

At first glance this might exclude young people with limited disposable income along with women with young families and limited family budgets. However, this is also potentially too simplistic. We may be able to identify two distinct customer personas, although they may be linked. One customer persona could be those with substantial disposable income who have strong ethical and environmental views who are willing to pay a premium for products that match their view of the world. If the product range is designed to be durable and high quality then this may also attract a different persona that is looking for value for money rather than a rapid turnover in their wardrobe. This may start to bring in those on limited budgets but who can see the benefit of high quality products. And so the marketing process develops and expands and evolves. Customers and their thinking do not stand still and successful businesses are those that recognise changes in attitudes, culture and even underlying beliefs.

Selling
Once you've developed a clear specification for your product or service and identified your target customers along with a pricing structure it's time to start selling. This is when the real hard work starts.

Many entrepreneurs try to start selling before they've sorted out the basics. They then find they don't have realistic responses to the questions from potential customers. At best you waste a lot of time, at worst you lose potential sales and damage the credibility of the business. Here are the basics you need:

Terms and Conditions (T&Cs)
These tell the customer what they can expect from you and what you expect from them. It is very important that these are provided to the customer before any work is done. The T&Cs form part of your contract to supply goods or services. They should be provided with a quotation from which an order is generated. Even with one click online sales there are T&Cs which often require you to click a box to say you have read and accepted them. Many people don't bother to read them and just tick the box – but this is part of the contract which is made when the order is placed at the next stage.

T&Cs should anticipate as many possible scenarios as possible – this is why they usually look long, legal and complicated. I'm not a lawyer so won't get into the legal aspects but some of the basics will include:

Payment terms
Returns policy
Delivery terms
Product guarantee details

How to resolve disputes
Use of personal data (GDPR)

A good starting point is to check out some of the T&Cs you have ticked in the past and those that go with products and services you have bought in the past.

It is critical to check out the T&Cs of your suppliers. The delivery terms and guarantee details may be vague and open to dispute. Not good if you are dependent on the supplies for your own sales.

Product/Service specification

This tells the customer what they can expect in terms of the product or service. Sometimes the requirements are mandatory for products such as chemicals, electrical equipment etc. You need to do sufficient research to ensure that you are operating legally and safely. The penalties for not complying with the rules can be quite tough.

A good example of potential problems is highlighted by the recent (2021) product problems with Peleton[11] the maker and supplier of gym equipment. At the time of writing the issues are still on-going but it appears there are problems with the user instructions and the safety of the equipment. The initial response from the company was also problematic. Sadly the alleged misuse of the equipment resulted in the death of a child.

Pricing Structure

Much of this is determined by the nature and type of product or service (or combined) – many products have significant service elements such as customer support. These can be critical in building customer loyalty, developing the brand and stimulating repeat/follow on sales. But this always comes at a cost. If this is not factored in at the outset then the entrepreneur sees the most basic customer service as an erosion of profits. This can lead to poor service (or none at all) which in turn leads to unhappy customers, negative comments on social media and sales can stall. This is not a good way to get traction (see later in this chapter).

There is a great temptation to price low in order to encourage customers to make a purchase. This often results in problems downstream because it is much more difficult to increase prices to realistic levels than it is to reduce them. There are many factors to take into account. If you are providing an existing product or service then there will be price pointing issues where customers expect to pay a certain amount and the business has to differentiate in order to win market share. Essentially you are trying to take business away from other players in the market. Differentiation then often comes down to quality of both product and service and/or price. Sometimes there are creative ways to create differentiation and to make the business stand out from the competition. Sometimes the start-up status can be used in a positive way to attract those that might be bored or dissatisfied with current product or service offerings. This often provides a good opportunity to start to build and develop the brand.

A new product or service faces different challenges as the potential customers need to be educated as to why your business might be relevant to their needs and to convince them that it's worth trying the product or service. Sometimes this may require some form of promotion to encourage usage and adoption and this can include a free trial period for products such as software. Again, this needs to be handled carefully as there is a risk of reducing the apparent value of the product or service in the eyes of the customers. In some personal service areas such as hairdressers, coffee shops et cetera there is scope for introducing loyalty card schemes which encourage repeat purchases.

In business to business situations an initial product trial may be appropriate and pricing issues may be supplemented by longer term contract offers which can incorporate price discounts on repeat purchases over contractual periods. This reflects the cost volume opportunities which are explained in Chapter 5.

All of these ideas reflect the importance of understanding customer needs, segmentation and the strength of competition. There are also issues about possible limitations on supply and the tangible benefits to the customer.

With a new product or service pricing becomes more problematic particularly if there are no competitive pressures. In these situations it is important that there is a clear vision and strategy for the future which anticipates the real costs of launching, supporting and developing the product or service and looks realistically at the product life cycle. Bear in mind that product life cycles are generally getting shorter as the pace of technological change accelerates and customer expectations develop.

If we look at the extreme situation of a new business which has developed a new market for a brand new product how would we approach the pricing issues?

The issues are:

Getting the product accepted

Maintaining a market share in the face of competition (competition can be significant from alternative products which are not the same, ie substitutes)

Making a profit

When a new product is launched on the market the pricing policy lies between the two extremes of market penetration and market skimming.

Market penetration pricing is a policy of low prices from launch in order to maximise penetration in the early stages. Short term profits are sacrificed for the sake of long term profits and market share. This policy will tend to discourage rivals from entering the market. The approach tends to shorten the initial period of the product life cycle bringing the growth and maturity stages as quickly as possible. This relates to a high elasticity of demand[12] for the product.

The business may deliberately build excess capacity and set prices low. As demand increases the spare capacity will be used up and unit costs will fall. There may even be scope for further price reductions as unit costs fall. Early losses (or low profits) will enable the business to dominate the market and have the lowest costs.

The above thinking is partly driven by the simple but important graphical representation:

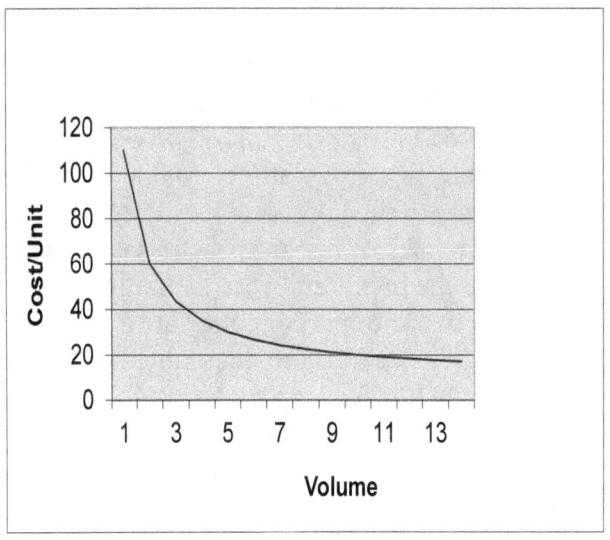

This is another example of the vital importance of understanding and controlling the cost base of the business. More of this in Chapter 5.

Market skimming is the achievement of high unit profits very early on in the product's life.

The business charges very high prices when the product is first launched.

There is heavy expenditure on advertising and sales promotion to win customers.

As the product moves through its product life cycle - growth, maturity and decline - prices are progressively lowered. The early profit is therefore skimmed off.

Skimming is suitable :

When the product is new and different

If demand elasticity is unknown (it is easier to reduce prices than raise them)

High initial cash flows are important at the possible expense of long term profit maximisation

To help to identify different market segments for the product each prepared to pay progressively lower prices.

The high initial prices may attract competitors who see the market as lucrative. The big risk comes from a competitor prepared to take the risks of market penetration which could immediately negate the premium of the skimming policy.

Between these two extremes of policy are a wide range of options. Most of these options are determined by the ability to identify clear segmentation opportunities, ie niches of the market which can be identified and targeted with a specific product offering and pricing policy along with meeting the needs and expectations of target customers.

A further consideration is evaluating the benefits of a new product to the customer. This can be illustrated by a fictitious example. A new paint is developed for jet passenger aircraft. The paint is lighter and thinner than conventional paints and improves the aerodynamic qualities of the aircraft. It also lasts twice as long between applications.

At cost price the value of the product for each painting of an aircraft is £10,000. What do you charge for it?

Bear in mind:

The cost of alternative (competitive) products.

There is a 2% reduction in fuel cost for the aircraft.

Painting a jet takes 6 days and needs to be done at least once per year with conventional paint.

Would £100,000 per application be expensive or cheap? What would be the short and longer term implications of your chosen pricing strategy?

Let's consider some of the hard facts:

The market size is well known, there are a relatively fixed number of planes in operation and these are added to and subtracted from as planes age and are replaced and passenger numbers and routes rise (or fall).

Airlines only make money when planes are in the air so minimising downtime is critical to them.

Fuel is one of the biggest costs in flying a plane as well as being one of the biggest environmental factors.

Now let's consider the offering. Do we just manufacture the paint? If we do we need to sell through painting contractors, the airlines and/or their maintenance contractors and even the plane manufacturers. This is important as it helps us identify the customer persona.

In this situation we are simply selling a product with a warranty and technical specification data and application instructions.

Pricing is likely to be fairly straight forward with a list price for, say 25 litre drums, with an opportunity for volume discounts on individual purchases as well as discounts for long term supply contracts.

You might find that some installation contractors want exclusive agreements so they can expand their own market share. A high selling price provides opportunities for discount deals based on volume and reliable customer orders.

If we provide a full service of manufacturing and applying the paint then we have to build in the labour and equipment costs of applying the paint and preparation of the plane. Warranties become a little more complex because we are providing a "full service" and so we take full responsibility for the finished painted plane.

Even with the full service provision we may use third party contractors for painting in order to increase our capacity. Considering the Finance material in Chapter 5 we will probably treat the third party contractors as a variable cost on each contract.

All of these issues must be reflected in the Terms and Conditions of supply as well as the Product/Service Specification and the actual contract for each job.

There are no simple solutions but I hope this example highlights the various opportunities and methods for getting a product/service to market – and making money.

Traction

Traction is a key part of selling and also demonstrating that a business is relevant to a potential investor – at any stage of development. Traction drives growth.

Traction links to the business model. Think of your idea as a vehicle – large or small – with wheels that are in contact with the ground. The vehicle has an engine and gearbox as well as a steering and breaking mechanism. How well the vehicle performs depends on a number of factors such as the surface over which it travels and how well the wheels grip.

A large, powerful vehicle on small wheels with bald tyres in a muddy field will just get wheelspin regardless of how much the engine revs. Indeed, the more power is transmitted to the wheels the more they will just spin. There is no traction.

A skilful driver may be able to coax it along a bit but it will always underperform its potential. Put it on a tarmac road and change the wheels and it might outperform any other vehicle.

Consider the road surface is your external environment or your market place. The wheels are the way you engage with the market place. Unless these are compatible the engine, gearbox and steering have little or no impact on moving the vehicle – in fact they can be part of the problem.

Don't forget the driver – that's you, the entrepreneur.

Change the wheels to big, deep treads, change the drive from two to four wheel drive, slow down the revs and the vehicle has traction.

Traction is the impact you have on your external environment. It reflects how well you've configured your business model to meet the needs of your target markets and your customers.

Take this thinking back to the business model. What is your vehicle designed to do and how does it achieve it? Are there other vehicles trying to push you off the road or block your progress – competitors?

An investor looks for how this model works. Much of the traction is generated by the management team and their credibility. They have designed the vehicle and should know how to drive it in varying conditions.

This forms a major part of any investor pitch but should go beyond the initial dream. It always helps if you can demonstrate the practical implementation – what have you sold, to whom and for how much? How can these initial sales be developed, added to and expanded?

One of the reasons why technology based businesses can attract very high early valuations is they have strong traction which can give them both speed and penetration. Businesses such as AirBnB[13] are a good example of a relatively simple business model, a strong technology base supporting it and great traction. The following chart shows the growth rate and traction.

A well established model for explaining how a new product or service gains traction is provided by diffusion of innovation model[14]:

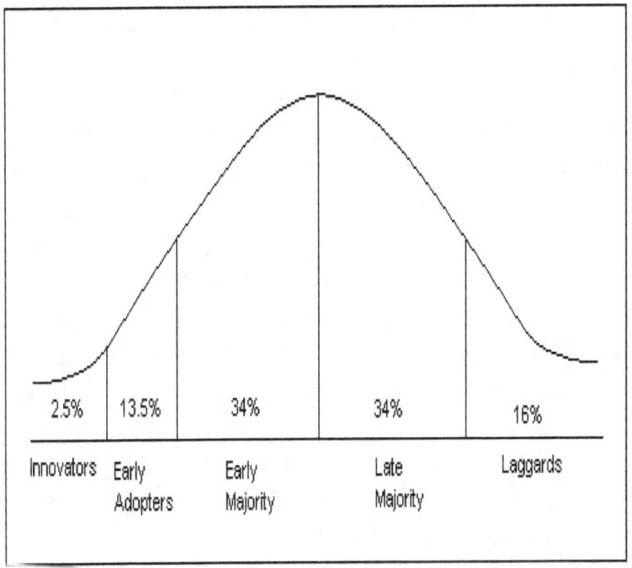

With any new product or service you need the Innovators who are curious and willing to take a risk. If you get these on board then you can start to sell to the early adopters. This is where the traction issues really come into play – you need good traction to get into the early majority.

Watch the Simon Sinek video[15] to understand the idea of "crossing the chasm" to get mainstream approval or acceptance of your product or service.

https://www.ted.com/talks/simon_sinek_how_great_lead ers_inspire_action/transcript?language=en

Is there a magic formula or prescription to work out your traction? The simple answer is no. Every situation is unique

– that's why you're an entrepreneur. I hope all the material in this book helps you to work out your own magic formula which will set you apart from your competitors.

All of the above takes a fairly traditional approach to developing a business and can also apply to mature businesses.

Eric Ries's book, the Lean Startup, takes things a bit further and highlights the importance of trial and error and learning from mistakes.

He promotes the idea of launching a "Minimum Viable Product" (MVP)[16], as a fast track way to test customer reaction. This is a great approach as it breaks down the inward looking thinking process that is highlighted throughout this book as a common cause of failure. The principle is quite simple:

The entrepreneur has an idea and believes this is the greatest idea ever developed – but this is just the opinion of the entrepreneur. Only when it is exposed to real customers can this belief be proven, challenged or broken. Ries explains the need to respond to this feedback quickly by reinforcing the approach, pivoting in a new direction or just closing it down and trying something different.

This fits with many of the ideas and suggestions put forward in this book and helps to underpin the whole meaning of innovation.

A book worth reading is Daniel Pink – To sell is human[17], which presents some great ideas and examples of effective selling.

Chapter 5 - Finance Essentials

Warm up Question:
What are the important financial issues that you need to be confident with as an entrepreneur?

Many entrepreneurs have a blind spot – lack of clear understanding about the essential elements of finance. This is not the same as bookkeeping or preparing accounts – these are just the established processes of 'keeping count' of the transactions.

Financial management (or the essentials) is about understanding cost structure, pricing and the impact of volume on profitability (or lack of it).

The approach I adopt with all start-up businesses (and some established ones) is to keep it very simple and focus on the key issues. Often the reality can be more complicated but if you understand the core principles then it is much easier to cope with the complexities.

Let's start with the absolute basics – the two types of cost in every organisation:

Fixed costs and variable costs.

It's important to define these very clearly:

Variable costs are those costs that vary in direct proportion to output – if you don't produce anything then you don't incur the costs. This is based on the "matching principle" used in compiling the Profit and Loss account or Income Statement. The Cost of Sales (Variable Cost) matches the Sales Revenue – so only the cost of sales which is used in generating the Sales Revenue is counted.

In the same way:

Fixed costs are those costs that do not vary with output – they are incurred regardless of the volume of output.

The definitions are important as it creates clarity and avoids simple descriptions such as "Overheads" etc. This helps us when we look at different types of business.

For example, a hotel uses electricity to heat and light the building, run computers, ovens, freezers, refrigerators……. The Sales Revenue of a hotel comes from renting rooms, feeding customers etc. While a busy hotel will use more electricity than an empty one there is unlikely to be a direct and proportional relationship – you can't just turn heating on room by room, ovens need to be kept hot and freezers cold regardless of customers.

On this basis electricity is usually regarded as a fixed cost – it is more fixed than variable.

A steel mill uses electricity to heat furnaces and run the rolling mill and so there is a direct relationship between the electricity consumption and the output of the steel mill. This would indicate that in this context electricity is a variable cost.

Before the "technical experts" start arguing about the technical merits of the simple example above remember that the purpose is to separate fixed and variable costs for the purpose of the analysis that follows. There will always be judgement in deciding how to classify costs - the important issue is to be consistent and understand how you are making the decision.

Why is this important and how do we use this knowledge and understanding?

If we take an imaginary product that is made out of components which are bought in by the Company.

These components will be a variable cost. The variable cost may also include the packaging – boxes, shrink wrap, pallets etc which are used in the production and shipping of the product. Direct labour may also be included as long as it is dedicated to this specific production process. Many small businesses have very flexible workforces so it's not always possible to be precise – this is where judgement comes in and explains why labour is often excluded from the variable cost.

An important feature of variable cost is that it's usually quite easy to identify a cost with each unit of production. For example, we will be able to calculate the cost of each component part even if we purchase in large batches – say 1000 at a time. Even the cling film and pallet costs can be calculated back to the cost for each product produced and shipped.

Fixed costs are difficult to allocate to a single product or unit of output. Fixed costs are often time based or linked to overall consumption. For example, rent is usually on a monthly or annual charge. Insurance is often the same etc.

This raises an interesting aspect of the definitions:

Variable costs may be relatively fixed! It is quite common to negotiate a price with a supplier that is fixed for a period of time, often based on anticipated volumes.

In the same way fixed costs may have a degree of variability. There may be seasonal fluctuations in energy consumption due to temperature and fixed costs may still vary with additional usage – for example a marketing campaign.

Let's say our figures look like this:
Variable cost = 60 pence per unit produced
Fixed Costs = £400 per month
Selling price = £1.00 per unit sold

A simple calculation shows:

Sales Revenue £ 1.00
Cost of Sales (Variable cost) £ 0.60
Gross Profit £ 0.40 (Sales Revenue − Cost of Sales)
Fixed Costs £400 per month

An important financial management tool is Break Even Analysis. The above information tells us:

Break even = Fixed Costs divided by Gross Profit per Unit

Therefore Break Even in this example is:
= £400 / £0.40
= 1000 units per month

This is the most basic business model but helps us to understand the viability of any business idea. If our market research (See Chapter 4) shows that sales above 1000 units per month at £1 per unit are feasible then we might have a viable business model – but there are lots of other issues to consider as we will see as the book progresses.

It may seem obvious but once we get past Break Even sales every unit of Gross profit translates directly into Operating Profit. For example, Sales of 1001 units in the month will result in an operating profit of £0.40. This highlights the way that variable costs go with each unit of sales. It also highlights an important feature of fixed costs – they don't increase with volume, until you reach the capacity of the existing production/output process.

The whole process can be presented graphically as shown below. All of these templates are available on the Website (www.changing-odds.com) and are fully interactive so you can try out "what if" scenarios.

UNITS	0	200	400	600	800	1000	1200	1400	1600	1800	2000	
FIXED COSTS	£400	£400	£400	£400	£400	£400	£400	£400	£400	£400	£400	£4,400
VARIABLE COST	£0	£120	£240	£360	£480	£600	£720	£840	£960	£1,080	£1,200	£6,600
TOTAL COST	£400	£520	£640	£760	£880	£1,000	£1,120	£1,240	£1,360	£1,480	£1,600	£11,000
SALES VALUE	£0	£200	£400	£600	£800	£1,000	£1,200	£1,400	£1,600	£1,800	£2,000	£11,000
												£0
PROFIT/LOSS	-£400	-£320	-£240	-£160	-£80	£0	£80	£160	£240	£320	£400	£0

VAR COST/UNIT	£0.60
SP/UNIT	£1.00
FIXED COSTS	£400

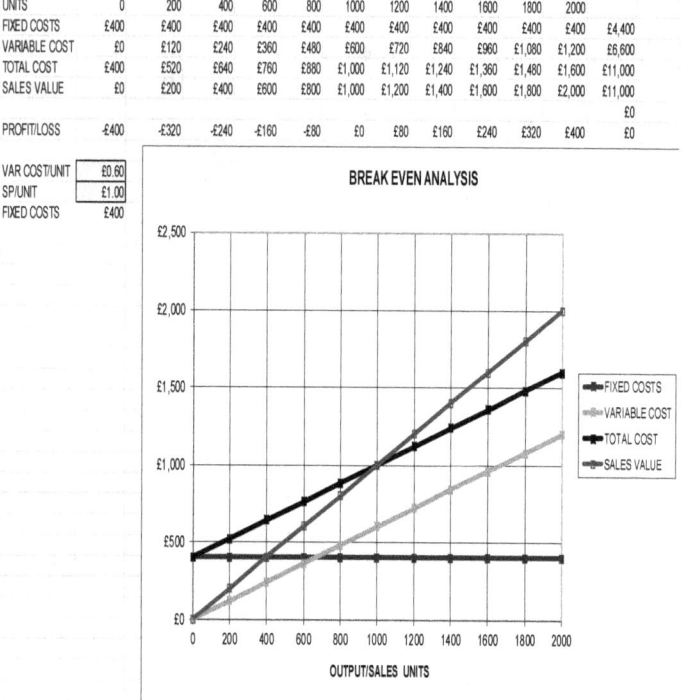

This enables us to consider the relationship between cost and volume. Let's take an extreme situation:

If we make and sell just one unit in a month the total cost of that unit is £400 plus £0.60. Let's develop this further:

Units Made and Sold	Fixed Costs	Variable Cost	Total Cost	Cost per Unit
1	£400	£0.60	£400.60	£400.60
2	£400	£1.20	£401.20	£200.60
4	£400	£2.40	£402.40	£100.60
8	£400	£4.80	£404.80	£ 50.60

The simple example demonstrates how variable costs are linked to every unit of output/sales while the impact (cost) of fixed costs is diluted (reduces) as volume increases. Again, this can be demonstrated graphically and we get a Cost/Volume curve by expanding the numbers:

Variable Cost	100	200	300	400	500	600	700	800	900	1000	1100	1200	1300	1400
Fixed Cost	10000	10000	10000	10000	10000	10000	10000	10000	10000	10000	10000	10000	10000	10000
Total Cost	10100	10200	10300	10400	10500	10600	10700	10800	10900	11000	11100	11200	11300	11400
Volume	10	20	30	40	50	60	70	80	90	100	110	120	130	140
Cost/Unit	1010	510	343	260	210	177	153	135	121	110	101	93	87	81

Variable Cost/Unit	10
Fixed Cost	10000
Opening Volume	10
Steps Volume	10

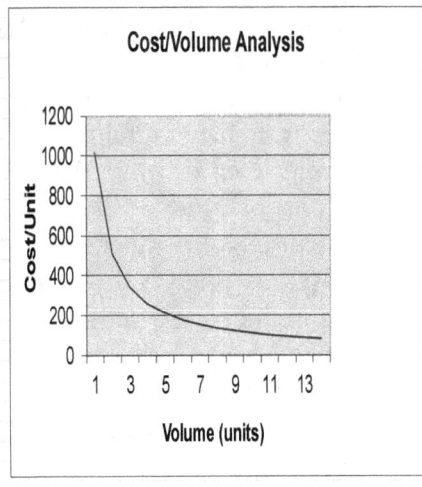

The impact of different Cost/Volume relationships can be important in all aspects of the business – negotiating prices with customers, discounts from suppliers and the volumes associated with any deals and contracts.

Taking the above example and assuming we are currently selling 100 units/week of the product as represented in the Cost/Volume diagram. Remember, this is a simple example that just shows the cost per unit. It does not include the profit element or mark up.

The current sales are to a range of small customers who are regular buyers. We are approached by a potentially big customer who we've been pursuing for some time. They want to buy 100 units per week of this product with a guaranteed 12 month contract and the potential for additional sales. It's no surprise that they want the best price and are talking to our main competitors.

Given our knowledge of the Cost/Volume relationship, what is our scope for price negotiation (reduction) without having a negative impact on our profitability. Put simply what is the impact of the additional order on our Cost/Unit and how much of this can we use in our price negotiation?

We can see from the diagram that our cost per unit at 100 units (our current level of output) is £1010. If we win the order then our cost per unit falls to £510 – a simple fact based on the cost structure. Remember this reflects the cost per unit to us – not the selling price to the customer.

We could reduce our selling price by the full cost reduction from the increased volume without having a negative impact on the business. I'm not suggesting we go this far but the important factor is that we enter the sales negotiation with clear and accurate information on our costs. There are other factors to consider such as whether we have the capacity without adding to fixed costs – but let's assume we have the capacity available.

If we win the order with a price reduction of £300 per unit our profits go up – we've just increased our operating profits by £210 per unit on the new sales.

But what if we "give away" the whole £510 cost saving per unit? Does the operating profit stay the same, go down or go up?

First thoughts might say the operating profits stay the same – but they actually increase. Why?

You now have sales of 200 units per week with a unit cost of £510 per unit. This is reflected in the selling price to the new customer, but you are still selling to your original customers at the "old price" based on a costing of £1010 per unit – so you make a premium profit on these original sales.

Sure, over time prices will even out but you should always use the cost/volume analysis to understand and drive your sales negotiation strategy.

Another reminder that this is a simple example to demonstrate some basic business principles around financial management.

Every product/service will have a different cost/volume profile. Consider the following different scenario:

Variable Cost	100	200	300	400	500	600	700	800	900	1000	1100	1200	1300	1400
Fixed Cost	100	100	100	100	100	100	100	100	100	100	100	100	100	100
Total Cost	200	300	400	500	600	700	800	900	1000	1100	1200	1300	1400	1500
Volume	10	20	30	40	50	60	70	80	90	100	110	120	130	140
Cost/Unit	20	15	13	13	12	12	11	11	11	11	11	11	11	11

Variable Cost/Unit	10
Fixed Cost	100
Opening Volume	10
Steps Volume	10

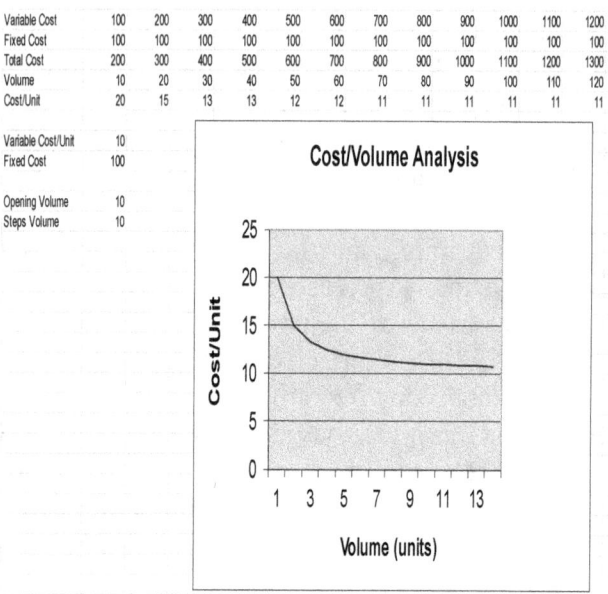

A similar scenario as before except we're selling 500 units/week to a range of customers. We're approached by a major potential customer wanting to offer an annual contract for 500 units/week.

They want a minimum reduction in our current price of £3.00 per unit in order to secure the order.

As you can see from the chart the impact of this order is only a reduction in our cost/unit of £1.00 per unit. At this level of output the graph goes "flat" the impact of volume on cost per unit is negligible so that asking for a bigger order doesn't improve the cost issue.

What do we do? Turn the order down as it will have a negative impact on our operating profit? That's too simple – and how many entrepreneurs want to turn away business particularly for existing products with no additional fixed costs?

Remember that the shape of the curve depends on a range of factors and all our suppliers are subject to the same "rules". What if we went to each of our suppliers and asked them for a new price based on us doubling our purchase with them. This is an attractive offer for any business.

If we then revised our cost structure the shape of the curve changes and we may see greater scope for price reduction. Go to the website and access the template to see how the numbers change.

While these examples are quite simplistic they should demonstrate the dynamic nature of cost, price and volume and the importance of understanding the relationships – and not guessing.

Supermarkets use these basic principle all the time with promotions – BOGOF – buy one, get one free and similar incentives to sell more. In most cases the price reduction is passed back to the supplier "encouraging" them to squeeze their own supply chains.

It's interesting to consider where the farmer goes to handle this type of negotiating pressure.

It is important to maximise variable costs at start up – and beyond and keep fixed costs to a minimum where possible.

At start up most businesses face uncertain sales – they are usually starting from zero and may be over-estimating how long it will take to achieve break even. Remember the comments in the Introduction about how businesses fail. We can use some of these basic financial management tools to help reduce the risk to the business.

Remember the basics about fixed and variable cost – you pay fixed costs regardless of output while you only incur variable costs when you produce and sell something. With uncertainty around output and sales it is always wise to keep fixed costs as low as possible for as long as possible. You can demonstrate this with the Break Even template to show the impact on Break Even by increasing fixed costs. You can access the interactive template in the Website (www.changing-odds.com).

Examples of turning fixed costs into variable costs are many and include:

Outsourcing elements of production

Outsourcing distribution

Sub-contracting labour

Sub -contracting software development

Yes, you may pay a premium over in-house provision but you only pay for the service when you need it. As sales increase you can evaluate each element to see when/if it is cost effective to bring it in house.

You should also think about optimum levels of purchases. As we've seen volume discounts are always a possibility but you need to take into account the cash flow implications of large scale purchases. The reduced costs may increase profits, but the real challenge is the working capital of having high stock levels which have to be paid for out of cash flow. Getting the balance wrong can be fatal and is often called "over-trading" – cash going out of the business is faster than cash coming in even when sales and profits look good.

Over the years I have come across many examples of good and bad practice when starting a business.

Some years ago I was approached by a manager in a client business who wanted to branch out on his own. There was an agreement with the client that this was acceptable and I was asked to help. At the time there was a lot of EU support available in the UK to encourage and support start-ups particularly in depressed areas.

The business model looked realistic with a new approach to a traditional food product. There were four company directors along with the manager (who became MD). They asked me to help produce a business plan and develop a funding bid for EU support. Over the next 3 months the plan was developed and a substantial grant was gained from the EU to rent a factory, buy machinery (second hand), set up the offices and infrastructure and employ a workforce. This grant aid enabled the directors to approach their bank for additional financial support for working capital – but with personal guarantees.

The factory opened, staff employed, equipment installed – all good to go.

As a freelance consultant I was not surprised to be thanked and told that they were fine on their own now – but they were also getting support from their accountants.

I arrived at the factory for a final visit. I knew they were in trouble before I parked the car in the car park. There in the car park were four brand new, top of the range executive cars – one for each director. Yes, they were leased – for cash flow purposes but the cash flow going out was still there on a month-by-month drip as the losses accumulated.

Ten months later the business folded having burnt through several hundred thousand pounds of funding and never achieving break even. The directors had had the "pleasure" of driving a top of the range car for a few months. At the end the bank called in the overdraft and all directors lost significant personal assets – as directors not shareholders – as they had signed asset backed personal guarantees. For one it cost his house and his marriage.

Lesson: Don't reward yourself until you're certain of success – in this case at least getting to break even and reducing the dependency on the bank debt.

Post script: Over the following few years the product idea adopted by this start-up was developed by other start-ups and became the new standard for this product. The approach is now responsible for a large market share in this sector of the food industry along with the high level of profits.

The Lesson: It doesn't matter how good the business idea if you don't get the financial essentials and the management right then you increase the risk of failure.

Several clients have developed highly successful businesses by understanding the links between, price, cost and volume. This can be one of the most effective drivers of growth.

It's important to remember that all these issues integrate into the fundamentals of understanding your customers, effective marketing, knowing the competition, matching quality and service with customer expectations – in fact all the other elements in this book.

With all of this in place each time you add to your output/sales your unit cost falls. You can sit and just milk the profits which will increase – but only for so long. This is where having a clear long-term strategy becomes critical. You have to look into the future and realise that competitors will not just sit and watch – they will attack you in a variety of ways. How do you develop the strategy?

Don't just think that saying "Our strategy is to continue to grow and maintain profits" is any kind of realistic strategy.

Richard Rumelt[1], the respected author of Good Strategy/Bad Strategy would describe this as Bad Strategy.

There is no evidence to suggest this is feasible, there is no analysis or statement of how much growth or the specific level of profit required over a timeframe. A Good Strategy requires an assessment of how the profits are being achieved – the financial analysis from above will help here. It also requires a future plan of action with feasible objectives.

Perhaps the strategy should look like:

Each customer is assessed to understand their purchasing profile both now and in the future.

Is there scope to increase sales to each customer?

Can we stimulate increased sales by "recycling" some of the reductions in unit costs to offer price reductions in return for long term contracts and/or improved payment terms.

This defends against competitor attacks using price and helps to build a stronger relationship with each customer.

This is reinforced with a commitment to an annual review based around volume level, prices etc.

The above strategy should increase both sales revenue and profits – now we can look at investing in product improvements, value engineering, new product development.

Now we have a tangible strategy which everyone in the business can understand – and so they clearly understand what they are doing.

Again, let me stress, the examples are quite simplistic but why complicate things?

What about Unicorns?

As I've highlighted in the Introduction the vast majority of start-ups start quite small and many stay that way – either by design or they lack the skills or motivation to grow beyond a certain limit. There is nothing wrong with this. Indeed, the main focus of this book is on these types of businesses and the entrepreneurs that invent and guide them.

But what about the relatively small number of aspiring Unicorns – those businesses deliberately set up to grow very fast, dominate an industry – sometimes by creating a new one or disrupting an existing one and to achieve a $1 billion valuation within the first few years?

Is the approach proposed so far suitable. As always the answer is not simple – some features are the same or very similar while others require a different approach. This also impacts on the nature and scale of funding. The slow and steady organic growth of many start-ups, often funded internally or with limited external funding, is not an option for the Unicorn.

Let's start by considering a new mobile phone company. In order to attract just a single customer they need to invest in a significant infrastructure – masts, servers, satellite links, security, customer service systems etc. Even with this major initial investment the costs are likely to rise in relation to customers/usage in order to handle customer enquiries and provide increasing levels of facilities.

This means the cost volume curve can often be the reverse of the one presented earlier – cost/unit rises as volume increases. This usually means a high level of investor support with equity and other long term funding. The benefit to these investors is that once they reach the tipping point of break even, cash flow and profits can accelerate significantly.

The same principle can apply to many projects based on apps. Just to get the first customer requires significant investment in the software development, interface design and marketing. Many apps are based on linking a customer to a supplier, so there is a lot of work needed to build critical mass of each one to make the app both credible and worthwhile to the users.

Think of AirBnB, Uber, Deliveroo[2] and many others.

There is not the same investment needed for physical infrastructure as in mobile phones but there is a need for investment in the app design and software development. Many start-ups in this area follow a similar development path:

Initial recognition of a need which identifies potential customers/users.

Develop an outline of the app which requires some design and software skills.

Start to build a team to build this initial design into a working prototype that can be tested and validated.

If there is little or no funding in the business so the founder(s) need to persuade the people with the necessary skills to join the team. This can often involve deferred payment and/or share options which create the opportunity for major benefits downstream. Early stage seed funding may be available to support some of this development.

Pilot launch to prove the relevance and validity of the app (Minimum Viable Product)[3].

Pitch to mainstream investors to fund full scale roll out – this may be over several funding rounds.

Critical to each pitch is the ability to demonstrate traction – the ability to grow quickly and even dominate the industry or sector. This is more to do with the commercial aspects rather than the actual technology. But the technology is still important!

Many Unicorns have highly innovative ideas which are often targeting to disrupt established industries/markets.

On 31st August 2021 a trial started in California around the collapse of a Company called Theranos which claimed to offer a revolutionary testing system for medical conditions. The Company was started by a 19 year old college dropout, Elizabeth Holmes in 2003 and reached a valuation of $9 billion in 2015. She was hailed as the new Steve Jobs. It had many high profile people on its board of directors. It then collapsed losing investors around $700 million.

Elizabeth Holmes is facing criminal charges alleging fraud.

In simple terms it appears the technology did not work and it raises serious issues about the willingness of investors to pursue risky projects despite the lack of hard evidence.

Investors also need to do their research and remain objective.

Take a little time to reflect on your answer to the warm up questions and make some notes on how your ideas and thinking might have changed (or not) by reading this chapter.

Chapter 6 - Funding

Warm up Question:
How much money do you think you need in the first 12 months of your business venture and how will you use it?

Many people worry about the funding issues from the outset. I hope you realise that funding flows from building a complete picture business which will include:
the market
the customers
pricing, costing, payment terms, stock requirements, in fact the whole working capital scenario
capital requirements for equipment and infrastructure

It's also important to consider the time to reach breakeven and generate positive cash flow. Sometimes generating a positive cash flow is not possible and this will be reflected in the funding requirements of the business. It's important to recognise that cash flow is a critical requirement of the funding model. Any external funding has to be serviced either by payment of dividends from profits for shareholders or interest payments on debt. The capital growth of the business is a potential additional reward for shareholders. This gets us into areas such as rights issues and share buy-backs which go beyond the scope of this book. There are some important ratios to consider when assessing the important funding issues and we will look at these as part of this chapter.

Understanding both the scale of funding and the time to reach breakeven are fundamental reasons why businesses succeed or fail. These two factors are critical in understanding the level of capital required by the business both in start-up stage and as it grows. Remember we highlighted in the introduction that lack of capital is a significant factor in business failure.

The table and chart below represents a very simple but quite realistic model that demonstrates the link between cash flow and funding.

Funding Need Example based on cash flow

Period	1	2	3	4	5	6	7	8	9	10	11	12
Income						10000	10000	15000	20000	25000	30000	35000
Start up Expenses												
Product development	1000	1000	2000	1000	1000							
IP Costs				5000								
Web site			1000									
Start up inventory				3000	5000							
Brand Building			500	1000	1000							
Marketing				1000	1000							
Staff Costs	500	1000	1000	1000	2000							
Insurance etc		100	100	100	100							
Post Launch Expenses												
Staff						2000	3000	3000	3000	3000	4000	4000
Purchases and supplies						5000	5000	7500	10000	12500	15000	17500
Marketing						1000	1000	1000	1000	1000	1000	1000
Insurance etc						200	200	200	200	200	200	200
Travel						200	200	200	200	200	200	200
Total Expenses	1500	2100	4600	12100	10100	8400	9400	11900	14400	16900	20400	22900
Cash Flow	-1500	-2100	-4600	-12100	-10100	1600	600	3100	5600	8100	9600	12100
Cumulative Cash Flow	-1500	-3600	-8200	-20300	-30400	-28800	-28200	-25100	-19500	-11400	-1800	10300

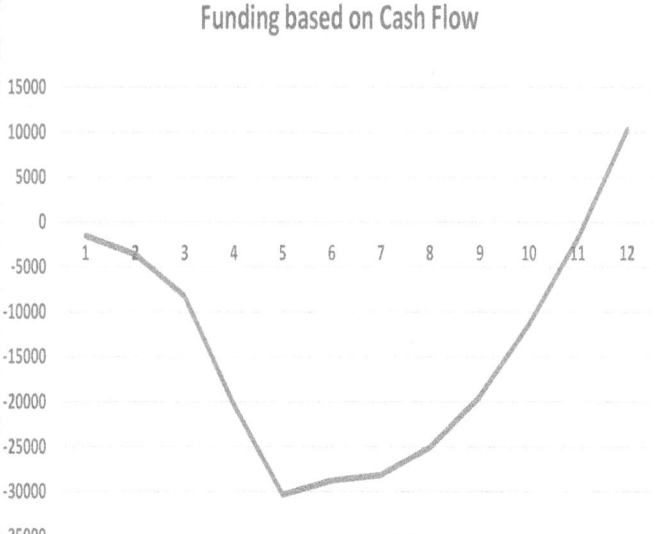

In this example we can see a very ambitious growth rate but it is still taking the whole year to get into positive cash flow. Many start ups take much longer to reach a positive cash flow – some never do and need to keep introducing extra working capital to support the business.

This helps to explain why profitable businesses can still go bust – they simply run out of cash. Indeed one of the big risks in a business, particularly in the early stage, is called over-trading. The business grows too fast to fund the working capital.

There are ways of solving this problem which we will look at later in this chapter.

The funding requirements flow from the forecast for balance sheet and cash flow which show how the resources of the business are utilised.

Let's start with the main sources of funding which are relevant and/or appropriate for your business.

Sole Trader

It's important to consider the context for you starting to work as a sole trader. If you've been made redundant or dismissed from your employment then the starting point is often your redundancy payment, savings that you may have, possibly small-scale loans, overdraft facilities along with credit cards.

You should be starting to see some of the implications as the loans and overdraft facilities will have personal liability along with the credit cards. Credit cards may attract interest rates of 30% or more and UK banks have recently raised overdraft rates to approaching similar levels even when these are approved overdrafts. Depending on credit rating a loan can attract interest rates from a few percent to similar rates for credit cards et cetera.

If you've not been made redundant and simply decided to go it alone then you have probably been planning your move into self-employment some time. The more you can work in a paid position while you get the business going the better as this is a source of funding. You need to be aware of potential conflict with an employer and so there are always risks involved. Check out your employment contract and any general rules that your employer enforces. You might be able to build up a savings pot and even take part-time work if you are forced to leave your main source of employment. All of these count as self-funding.

This highlights part of the limitation of self-employment as a sole trader. It is very difficult to scale the business. You are simply replacing an employed position and you carry all the risks associated with running a business with limits on the returns based on your hours of work. However, you have the freedom to work as you choose.

Partnerships

Partnerships are made up of a group of sole traders and so many of the issues highlighted above will apply to the partnership. However, there is a significant opportunity to pool resources and therefore create more opportunities for developing scale operations.

However, as we highlighted in the outline of partnerships in Chapter 2 it's important to have a written partnership agreement so there are no misunderstandings about the various resources and expertise that each partner brings to the partnership as well as the way that profits will be shared. It's also important to remember that a partnership has joint and several responsibilities for its liabilities.

Sole traders and partners only report to the tax authorities so their businesses can't be assessed by the public. This is one of the main reasons why they have no protection and accept all the risks of borrowing, contracts etc on a personal basis.

Limited Liability Partnerships

These are a hybrid between a partnership and a limited liability company. Essentially it allows partnerships to function as above but with limited liability protection which is in return for a greater degree of disclosure than a basic partnership. It is disclosure that is the key to accessing many sources of funding and enabling the business to scale up.

Limited liability companies

There are various forms of this legal structure within many countries. It is the accepted way to operate a business if you want to grow beyond being a sole trader and provides a range of benefits in return for filing annual accounts and providing a degree of transparency to the public – which includes suppliers, customers, investors, lenders etc.

A company can exist in perpetuity. There are companies that have been in existence for over 100 years and some have the shares held by members of the same family over this period. The features of a company limited by shares are:

Management flexibility. Shareholders have to appoint at least one director to manage the business. Most entrepreneurs will appoint themselves but there is scope to build a professional management team as the business develops. This can help with investors who are nervous about being dependent on a single person or a small team with little experience.

Greater financing potential. The requirement to publish accounts and shareholder and management structure gives investors and lenders greater confidence. This transparency can also help in negotiating trade terms with suppliers and customers.

Stability of market image. The permanence of the company as described above helps the business build a brand and create confidence with all stakeholders.

Measure of personal investor protection. The limited liability limits the risk and exposure of the shareholders to their share value. This is what they lose if the business fails. Be aware that directors have different legal responsibilities even if they are also shareholders. There is a dual legal personality.

All of this underpins this structure as the optimum way to raise finance to fund growth. Few investors and lenders are interested in simply funding a business for it to stand still. Suppliers will often offer better trading terms to businesses that they see growing – the logic is simple – there is a mutual benefit.

Directors/proprietors Funds

As you can see from the simple cash flow model at the start of this chapter most businesses start with an outflow of money which can be quite substantial before income starts to be generated. As outlined for the sole trader there is often a degree of self-funding in many start-ups when they are incorporated businesses. A sole trader can put money in and take money out without any accountability to anyone else. However, a limited company has to operate to different rules as the business has its own legal personality. Funds provided by the shareholders/directors over and above the share capital should be in the form of a Director's Loan. This must show on the balance sheet – the funds themselves are cash shown as a current asset which is balanced by a current or long-term liability or what the business has a responsibility to repay.

There can be issues around how such sources of funding are taxed particularly when the loans are repaid. Check out the local rules and seek professional advice.

Start-up loans

Many countries have agencies that support new and growing businesses with a range of grants and loans. Some of these agencies will focus on particular regions and/or industries. Many of these loans are the equivalent of personal loans but check out the range of options and the eligibility criteria in the country where you are based.

Since Covid many governments have provided additional support simply to help businesses survive. It's possible that some funding streams may continue for some time so keep checking what's available. Many of these schemes are government backed and can provide some quite generous terms compared to some sources of bank lending.

One of the challenges when applying for a start up loan is calculating how much to pitch for. There is often a maximum limit as well as conditions associated with rules on state aid – mainly associated with European funding streams. If this maximum is below your requirements you may struggle to convince the lender that it will be sufficient so you may need multiple sources of finance.

It is also important to be realistic about how much you really need. You should always include a contingency amount in case you underestimate some of the basics. For example, two months after you launch a competitor starts to undercut you on price. If you cut your prices it impacts on breakeven as well as cash flow – which means you need more funding. If you don't cut your prices then sales may grow slower than planned – again affecting cash flow as well as profitability.

Factoring

Factoring can be a very useful way of funding a business that is growing quite rapidly and where customers have payment terms in excess of 30 days.

The simple scenario is that you agree with a specialist factoring business to finance your invoices in return for a fee.

You sell a product to a customer and immediately raise an invoice. You provide the factoring company a copy of the invoice and they immediately transfer around 80% of the invoice value your bank account so you get immediate access to the bulk of the invoice value. You get the balance of the invoice when the customer pays the full invoice value to the factoring company. A fee (%) is deducted from the invoice value as well as fixed charge calculated on your annual turnover.

There are a number of rules that apply in most situations:

A single customer can't represent more than a specified percentage of your total turnover – usually around 25-30%.

If the customer goes beyond 90 days then full value of that invoice is deducted from the overall factoring facility.

The factoring company effectively "buy" your invoice and have full responsibility for collecting the customers payments. This loss of control for the business selling the products can sometimes lead to problems with customers if the factoring company are over-zealous in collecting any overdue monies.

Factoring often has a reputation of being an expensive source of funding. The fees can be quite significant in total but if the business is growing at a steady rate with increasing levels of debtors then it can be a serious alternative to regular visits to the bank to re-negotiate an overdraft facility with all the associated fees and charges. You can also save money as you don't need to pay someone to chase customer payments – a time consuming and sometimes stressful job. Each overdraft re-negotiation usually comes with a fee and the option to change (increase) interest rates. It's also worth noting that many overdrafts can be called in with only 30 days notice.

Invoice discounting

Invoice discounting works in a very similar way to factoring but with some important differences. Invoice discounting is usually only available to businesses that have been trading for some time and have a well established customer base.

You retain ownership of all the invoices and have responsibility for collecting all the money. The Invoice Discount company use the value of the invoices as security for your borrowing against the invoice value. You have to be able to demonstrate effective systems to support the debt collection processes.

Many of the same rules apply and there may be special rules for specific businesses. Most of the support provided by factoring and invoice discounting is focused on product based companies who are selling a relatively simple product where customer disputes are rare. The range of services offered is constantly evolving and it's worth shopping around to find a provider that suits your precise needs. And always check the small print.

Crowdfunding

Crowdfunding has been developing rapidly over recent years and is becoming quite an important source of funding. It is still evolving with different structures but the basics focus on two main features:

Equity crowdfunding where individuals and institutions can subscribe to a share offer to help the organisation build a capital base to fund on-going development.

Pre-purchase crowdfunding where individuals help the development of new products and services by paying in advance of the product/service being available. This helps to finance the development process, production costs such as tooling, software etc.

There are a range of platforms that support crowdfunding proposals and many of these have specific themes which help to categorise different types of projects such as technology, arts, films etc.

At it's most basic a business will pitch on a platform for a specific amount of money with a time frame for people to subscribe – say 30 days. At the end of the time frame if the target has been reached then the business can draw down the money. If it falls short then the pitch fails and the business gets nothing. This is the original model and some platforms provide increased flexibility such as an option to extend the time frame under certain circumstances.

There is a sensible logic that falling short of the funding target means the business will be under-funded and therefore at an increased risk of failing.

The details of a crowdfunding pitch can be quite complex in terms of what is offered and incentives to encourage investors and purchasers with added benefits. This goes beyond the broad scope of this book.

However, as in any pitch the quality and focus of the business proposal is critical and can require some up front costs. It is normal to use a video to pitch the business idea supported by a full business plan with detailed financials. The quality of the video is vital and should have professional input. To get a good idea check out some of the pitches that are presented on some of the platforms.

Grants

Grants can be a great way to build the development stage of any business. They are often focused on Research and Development projects as well as capacity building. They are often funded by government agencies and managed by a variety of local organisations and sometimes linked to university research programmes. Finding the right ones requires quite a lot of research and then time and research to pitch for the funding.

There are also agencies that support social projects where the main focus is not profit but supporting communities and individuals who have needs that are not being met by the formal infrastructure. Again, finding the right sources requires further research and effort in presenting the right pitch.

It's important to remember that while this may appear to be "free money" there are often quite significant costs and time issues involved. The money has to be managed and accounted for which often requires setting up separate monitoring and accounting systems. There may also be a requirement for the business to contribute from their own funds. For example, a 60% grant will require the organisation to find the balancing 40% and there may be limitations on how this can be sourced. The detailed rules are quite critical and can be quite onerous.

Finally, don't forget the working capital implications. Sometimes there may be an up-front payment to kick start the project. This is great but future payments are likely to be paid after expenditure has been made and this can be quite a protracted process. The business has to fund this payment delay as the grant claim is usually based on paid invoices and expenses.

Again, the detail is critical.

Seed Capital

Quite simply this is capital to help get the business idea moving and growing. There are a variety of agencies offering seed capital often funded by government agencies as well as some financial institutions.

There are also increasing opportunities for peer to peer lending through a range of platforms. There are many options which can involve both equity and debt. Again finding the right package involves research and preparation.

Business Angels

Business Angels are wealthy individuals who are looking to invest in businesses usually in return for equity although there can often be a mix of equity and debt.

Understand the motives of a business angel – they want to make money from your business and are willing to take some risks in order to get a higher return than they can make from other investments. This means they are looking for growth businesses where there is a prospect of returns from dividends, interest on debt and capital growth.

This is a major commitment from both the business and the angel so it is critical that the relationship is clearly understood both in formal contractual terms and in the way the two will work together. It is likely that the angel will have a time frame in mind for exiting the business with a target valuation in mind and it is often wise to agree milestones for the journey.

The relationship details are important as some angels may want a passive role while others may have experience in similar businesses and can offer support in networking, mentoring and even technical advice as well as management and commercial inputs.

Venture Capital

There are specialist venture capital (VC) organisations who provide investments to start-ups as well as mature organisations. There are many organisations to choose from. Essentially a VC is a fund manager that takes investor money from individuals and organisations and looks for businesses to invest in with the opportunity for a higher rate of return than alternatives. The sources of funding will include government, pension funds, sovereign wealth funds and wealthy individuals. All are looking to have a high rate of return reflecting the increased risk of investing in businesses.

They all have a common objective – high growth rates in the business. What is high? While target rates will vary depending on the economic climate it is unlikely that a VC will be interested in a business which is projected to grow at less than 20% per annum (compound) over a five year period. This is quite a demanding target and helps to explain the very low success rate of businesses pitching for VC funding – less than 5%.

Private Equity

While the experts may argue with me the Private Equity (PE) sector is an extension of the Venture Capital sector. Indeed many PE organisations also operate as VCs.

This is the type of funding that may be attractive to potential Unicorns and is unlikely to be realistic for most start-ups.

Every element of funding can get quite complicated and is under-pinned by detailed contractual obligations. The purpose of this part of the book is to provide a general overview as the detail would build into a book in its own right.

The website that goes with this book explores some of these issues in more detail and will provide a platform for discussing various aspects of funding as well as helping to identify specific source for different areas. Visit www.changing-odds.com for more details.

Finally, there are signs that some investors are considering the ethical and environmental impact of their investment. Fund managers who manage VC and PE operations raise much of their money from savers – often pension funds – who themselves are custodians of the savings of ordinary people who are paying into pension plans. Increasingly the pension funds want to present their customers with the scenario that their pension contributions are not being invested in businesses that have poor ethical standards and damage the environment.

However, they still need to generate suitable returns so many of the core benchmarks continue to influence the investment decisions. This is an evolving part of the savings and investment industry.

There are some interesting and relevant articles and books on the topic and a worthwhile book is Nature's Fortune by Mark Tercek and Jonathan Adams1. The book highlights opportunities and examples of how business can generate financial returns by investing in nature with sustainable outcomes. It helps to quantify the benefits – which is always a necessity for investors.

Social Enterprise Funding

Organisations that are set up with a primary aim of benefitting society, the environment and communities can often access additional funding streams that are not available to purely commercial organisations.

The legal structure of these organisations is often an important factor in being able to access these funds – the funding agencies don't want to see grant funding being paid to shareholders as dividends.

Every country has different structures and rules. In the UK there various structures such as company limited by guarantee which can't pay dividends and community interest companies which can pay limited dividends under quite strict rules.

There are a range of sources of funds including the Big Lottery Fund, the Arts Council and specialist funds such as Esmée Fairbairn3 and John Muir Trust4 . These are just examples and there are many more – so do some research.

Social enterprises can also attract funding from angel investors, ethical investment funds (linked to private equity), crowd funding and conventional bank lending.

An alternative to actual funding is gaining support for the provision of assets. A local authority may have a building which is surplus to requirements but is costing money for security and maintenance. Sometimes these might be available for use by a social enterprise or charity at a very low (peppercorn) rent. This can be even more beneficial if the project links to community benefits.

Sponsorship from commercial organisations is also a way to support community projects in return for enhancing the reputation of the commercial organization. Be aware that some commercial organisations use this as a form of PR and even so called green washing.

However, these "partnership" projects are quite popular with both commercial organisations and social enterprises. There are many examples which can be researched. Business Fights Poverty6 is an umbrella organization that brings partners together and provides a platform for projects.

Accelerators

Over recent years there has been a lot of development in what are known as Accelerators. These are facilities where budding entrepreneurs can get together with all the resources they might need:

Office facilities with all the necessary technology even 3D printing, CAD systems etc.

Meeting facilities

Professional support for helping build the business such as legal help for Intellectual Property, contracts etc.

Access to mentors.

Access to early stage funding such as seed capital, angel investors and venture capital.

In the USA these facilities are well established and operate by giving the entrepreneur support for fast track growth often with the ultimate goal of an Initial Public Offering (IPO) where the founders and early stage investors can make substantial gains. This approach does not suit every business and there is a danger that the process is linked to a timetable that is unrealistic for many entrepreneurs and just becomes a box ticking exercise to prove to the funders that the entrepreneur has been taken through the recommended stages of the programme.

If you have a high growth business idea and can be totally committed then an accelerator may be the right thing – but shop around and find the one that suits you.

I have spent the last 10 years working on a freelance basis as a mentor at the Innospace unit at Manchester Metropolitan University. This is a business incubator rather than an accelerator. We deliberately let the entrepreneurs find their own pace and support them with mentoring, peer support from other businesses in Innospace, office facilities and a range of workshops and access to funding streams.

While this may not suit potential Unicorns it is a good approach for the vast majority of entrepreneurs who want to build and evolve at a pace that suits them.

Innospace2 itself does not provide grants or loans but we are able to assess and award small start up grants under the Santander Universities programme.

IPO

Finally, once you've built the business to a significant level of turnover and profit you can float or list the business on a stock exchange and sell shares to institutional investors and the public. This is a common "exit route" for the entrepreneur and the investors that have helped build the business.

The details of an IPO go well beyond the scope of this book but for some entrepreneurs this is the ultimate goal – but only for a few is it realistic.

There is no need to float all the shares – sometimes just floating 20% is sufficient to raise the new capital needed both for expanding the business and giving the founder and early investors a healthy return on their work.

There are strict rules on IPOs and these include the use of professional advisers – you can't just do it yourself. This comes at a high price and even a basic listing on, for example, the Alternative Investment Market (AIM) in the UK which is designed for smaller businesses, the fees can start as high as £500,000.

Chapter 7 - Making the business work

Warm up Question:
What is your business model – a short statement about why you exist and how you survive?

Up to this stage in the book we've been building the foundations from which a successful business can develop and grow. The real secret of success is to recognise and exploit the interactions of all the component parts. This is how you make the business work.

This is where we start to bring all the issues, information and evidence together.

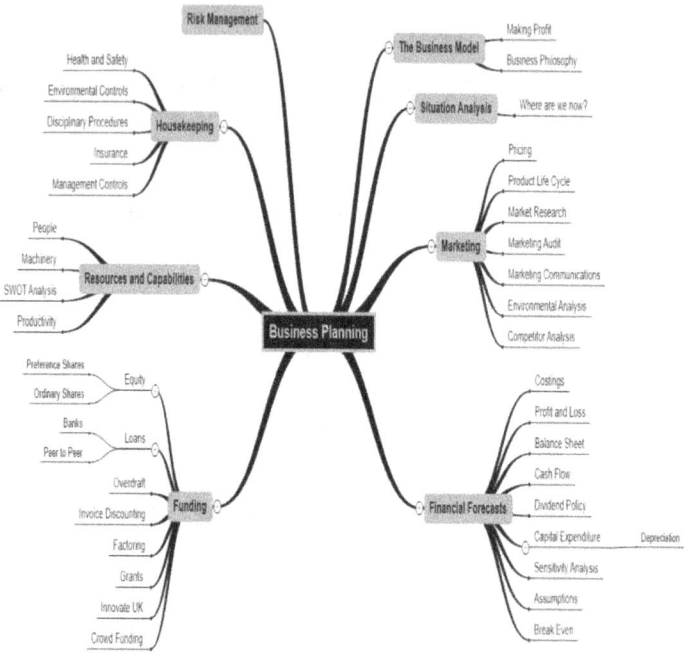

Don't be intimidated by this mind map. It is intended to provide a check list of things to consider and not everything will apply but you will need something under each main heading.

This can also provide a platform for any presentations you may make. It's important to remember that different audiences will need a different focus and content but it should all be consistent and honest – otherwise you may get muddled up.

By now you should have a good idea of the technical content for each heading such as working out the break even and linking it to the market potential and the costing and pricing. This in itself can highlight some of the sensitivities to aggressive pricing from a competitor, inflation and changes in interest rates. Changes in interest rates are often linked to inflation and can have a big impact not just because of changes (increases) to your own cost base but an impact on overall demand in the market place. This can be a double hit – usually negative.

Current note for 2021 – most major economies are injecting massive sums into public expenditure to help overcome the negative impact of Covid 19. This creates major opportunities in many industries as it is intended to stimulate demand, increase employment and GDP. However, some are warning about inflation rising with the possible impact on increases in interest rates. This is what central banks are in business to manage.

No one really knows what will happen – we may know in 2022 or beyond. The important issue for the entrepreneur is to understand that many of these factors are certainties – we just don't know how much or when the economy will shift. This is a real world issue and the entrepreneur who doesn't take the possibilities into account should not blame "bad luck" for any negative outcomes. This is where monitoring the external environment all the time is critical.

Perhaps the real skill is to be able to understand the relative certainties for example the demographic trends of aging populations in developed economies, poverty in parts of the world (including some developed economies), political instability in many parts of the world; there is a long list to keep an eye on. The successful entrepreneur is often credited with some mysterious insight about the way these factors interact and create opportunity. Some might call it good luck. The reality is that there is a lot of good scientific research to explain many of these successes.

Chapter 4 highlights some of this research but the real answer is quite simple - Stay curious! Chapter 8 builds on this research in developing strategy.

As you build each element in this picture you are starting to pull together the story which is your Business Plan. I'm not a fan of the templates used by many banks. They are necessary if you apply for various forms of funding but they often limit the scope of the business ideas.

It's important to recognise that a business plan serves many purposes and you may need several versions each focusing on a different aspect of the business. For example, an application for government support may focus on job creation or export potential. An application for a bank loan will focus on the ability to repay the capital and interest charges. Chapter 14 provides some further insights into the whole process of business planning.

The Academic/Researcher Issues

Many entrepreneurs start off from an academic and research background. This is highlighted with many technological developments and illustrates the importance of universities and other research institutions that drive progress in a range of technological, environmental and other areas of research and development.

The assumption that a great idea and research programme will inevitably attract funding and a commercially successful outcome is not borne out by much evidence. The reality is that many researchers seek perfection. Indeed, once an idea reaches fruition then it might create commercial gains but it might also effectively make the researcher redundant. This may seem an overly simplistic view but it underpins the thinking of many people involved in research and development. When you take it to commercialisation you have lost control and therefore you are no longer necessary. The solution is never let it go.

The real challenge for all research projects is to recognise the need to bring in commercial reality and to develop the ideas into a commercially sustainable product or service. This then creates the opportunity to use the revenue and the recognition from the success to fund new areas of research and development.

However for many researchers who have been brought up in a higher education environment where possession of knowledge is the key to progression and academic recognition then the idea of sharing knowledge is often difficult to accept.

The ultimate example of a major business failure based on this principle is the Xerox facility at Palo Alto. This establishment created some of the most innovative inventions and developments which they failed to exploit and which were simply recognised and developed by other organisations.

How do we overcome this problem?

The first step is to recognise the limitations researchers have in any entrepreneurial activity. They need to have the confidence to engage with commercially aware partners and individuals who can help them go beyond this idea of perfection. Perfection is a great idea but is rarely needed by actual customers.

It's important to recognise that the research and development can often develop four or five future iterations and developments in the technology. However, this is irrelevant if the customer does not need these future iterations. This takes us back to the principles of marketing and understanding what customers need and what their current requirements are in Chapter 4

You may be questioning why I've focused on the academic/researcher character. I've started here to highlight perhaps extreme characteristics that impact on many (if not all) entrepreneurs. In later chapters we look at developing these characteristics in more depth and considering what different types of entrepreneurs need in addition to their brilliant idea in order to succeed.

First I want to consider some basic ideas to provide a platform for some of the practical techniques discussed so far in the book.

Over the last 30-40 years an interesting model has been developed and utilised primarily for recruitment and job skills.

T Shaped skills were popularised by David Guest[1] in 1991 but the thinking was probably started in the 1980s with the term "T-shaped man" which was used internally by McKinsey & Company[2] for recruiting and developing consultants and partners, both male and female.

The idea is very simple:

> **The horizontal bar**
>
> This shows the breadth of knowledge

> **The vertical bar**
>
> This shows the depth of knowledge in a specific skill or area of expertise
>
> The narrower the bar the more specialised the person
>
> The depth of the bar shows the depth of knowledge – in this specialist area

The original thinking was to consider the horizontal bar to reflect the ability to interact with others, particularly those with different technical skills which in turn, it is assumed, results in integrating technical experts into multi-disciplinary teams with a broader range of skills available.

It's a great theory with some good practical applications but it can create issues for the entrepreneur. Starting with the academic/researcher it is common to find these people have great depth in the vertical bar but it is often quite a narrow bar and, importantly, the horizontal bar can be quite limited. This creates what is often called "myopia" in both the level of strategic thinking as described by Richard Rumelt[3] in Good Strategy, Bad Strategy and the way that alternative approaches and ideas to those of the entrepreneur are rejected as discussed by David Robson in the Intelligence Trap[4]. We will look at this in more detail in later chapters but at this stage I just want to highlight a common human characteristic:

Many people who are regarded (and regard themselves) as intelligent get trapped into biased thinking based on their areas of deep expertise and knowledge. They will argue against and often reject alternative views and ideas simply because they have not thought of them.

Overcoming this bias is a big challenge that we consider later in the book but let's start with some of the basic areas of understanding. For the entrepreneur let's consider the T shape as part of a grid to develop:

Level 3 Change	Level 2 Change	Level 1 Change	Central Core	Level 1 Change	Level 2 Change	Level 3 Change
		Leadership	Focus and Dedication	Research paper writing		
					Working with other Deaprtments	
	Team Work		Collaboration			
						Consider alternative approaches
Empower the Team			Curiosity			
Employ for commitment as well as knowledge and skills	Recruit to provide appropriate skills and resources	Acknowledge personal skills limitation	Core area of knowledge and research	Broaden the scope		Finding Partners with different approaches/theories
Delegate and monitor - not micro-managing	Invest in appropriate control systems to provide feedback	Understand the role of leadership - now and in the future	Develop the "doughnut" by looking at complementary techniques	Acknowledge the opportunities for new ideas	Understanding customer needs	Discussions with partners
	Develop Knowledge sharing culture	Accept criticism and embrace humility	Understand how the expanded view builds the business model		Sharing knowledge	Sharing knowledge
Stand back and watch the team perform		Reframe the model with the new insights	Re-evaluate the business model and overcome the myopia			Formal partner agreement
Start working "on the business" instead of "in the business"		What does the customer want/need?	Develop next level of research	Perhaps a new approach to commercialising R&D?	Expand the business model	Re-invent

It's important to stress that every grid will be different for different entrepreneurs and situations. The one above presents some examples for a typical research based entrepreneur project. This is not a static model and may start with some relatively limited ideas but the purpose is to encourage you, as the entrepreneur, to reflect on your ideas and recognise and accept problems, differences, weaknesses and then take action.

Don't expect to be perfect – you won't be, but learn from the mistakes and be prepared to re-invent yourself and your business model.

"Any company that succeeds at restructuring and re-engineering, but fails to create the markets of the future, will find itself on a treadmill, trying to keep one step ahead of the steadily declining margins in yesterday's businesses."
G Hamel, C K Prahalad

Chapter 8 - Developing a strategy

Warm up question:
What is a strategy and do you have one?

There are vast volumes of academic writings on strategy, lots of publications, MBA modules, executive training courses, consultant briefings..........

Just how practical and realistic are all of these offerings, suggestions and approaches.

I've worked with business schools on MBA programmes and helped boards of directors "develop" strategies. There can be a lot of value in understanding relevant strategy theory – but there is a lot of questionable material which is little more than common sense.

So do you spend months developing a strategy? I would strongly advise against too much detail and instead suggest a "quick and dirty" approach to developing a strategy – and then keep it constantly under review.

A good starting point is a single book – Good Strategy/Bad Strategy by Richard Rumelt[1]. This is perhaps the best book on strategy written in recent times. The title highlights the simplicity of the approach. I will use some of the ideas mixed with my own experience of developing an effective strategy.

A few years ago I ran a series of workshops to help small businesses progress from early stage to growth and sustainability. At the start of each session the delegates were asked to introduce themselves and their business. They were encouraged to highlight their key objectives, problems that were holding them back and even what they wanted from the business. One delegate described his truck security business which had a patented security system to prevent/detect unauthorised/illegal entry to large curtain sided lorries. This was a particular issue at the time as the UK was experiencing migrants getting inside vehicles. Drivers were facing heavy fines if an illegal migrant was discovered on their vehicle – regardless of whether they knew or not. This was a nice business idea with some clear potential that the owner recognised.

He explained the product, the market and some basic statistics. He also declared his strategy – to develop the business and then sell out within 5 years for at least £10 million. At the time he was about 30 years old.

The problem was that he didn't have a strategy – he had an aspiration, a hope, perhaps an objective. But there was no understanding of what was needed or how he could achieve this. He believed all he had to do was advertise the product in appropriate trade journals, get some good PR – sales would come in, he'd organise the supply chain and it would create a business valued at £10 million – that he could just walk away from.

Rumelt suggests that a good strategy contains three key elements[2]:

A diagnosis that defines or explains the nature of the challenge. A good diagnosis simplifies the often overwhelming complexity of reality by identifying certain aspects of the situation as critical

A guiding policy for dealing with the challenge. This is an overall approach chosen to cope with or overcome the obstacles identified in the diagnosis.

A set of coherent actions that are designed to carry out the guiding policy. These are steps that are co-ordinated with one another to work together in accomplishing the guiding policy.

Rumelt goes on to consider a fundamental question needed in any diagnosis (credited to John Mamer of UCLA Anderson School of Management)[3] which drives the diagnosis:

"What's going on here?"

Distilling this for the truck security business owner might have gone something like:

Most small business owners are key components in developing and growing the business. To walk away after 5 years with £10 million requires a recognition that the owner must reduce/eliminate this dependency. This is the initial challenge – not an afterthought.

There must be a clear policy on pricing, costs and potential competition. What if an alternative technology is developed? Is the system still relevant? Are there alternative applications that can be developed. These (and others) form part of the diagnosis.

Fundamental to the guiding policy is to recognise from the outset the need to build a professional and competent management team so that the owner can extract himself from the business. This can't wait for 5 years, it has to be developed from the outset so that there are appropriate systems, processes and controls in place. It also provides a platform for the culture in the business which includes the willingness of staff to take responsibility and even recognise the risks and how to manage them. This will probably take all of the 5 years – starting at the beginning of the business.

All of this comes at a cost which will impact on the profits – particularly in the short term. This reflects investment in the business by the owner or the need to bring in an investor in the early stages. This in turn will impact on the timing and scale of the exit package for the owner.

All of the above needs much more detail as well as continuous monitoring but the outcome is more likely to be a sustainable business with the potential for the owner to achieve a realistic exit. At this stage the £10 million in 5 years is no more than a nice idea.

As the above strategy evolves it will become clear that further options will develop, for example:

A competitive product may reduce sales but may also broaden the scope of the market.

Prices and margins may need to reduce in order to maintain sales growth as competition increases.

Changes in border security systems and even legislation may change the need for the product – either positive or negative.

The only certainty is uncertainty. The £10 million in 5 years may be a good discussion topic at a dinner party but it isn't a strategy.

Rumelt adds the thought that good strategy is not just "what" you are doing, it is also "why" and "how" you are doing it.

This takes me to another good source of ideas on both strategy and the way you think about the business. When working with aspiring and actual entrepreneurs at bootcamps and workshops I often play a video by Simon Sinek – Start with Why[4]

https://www.ted.com/talks/simon_sinek_how_great_leaders_inspire_action?language=en

This summarises the ideas in his book – Start with Why.

I encourage entrepreneurs to follow this advice – if only to avoid the dreadful and boring approach to business plans which start with a long and painful technical description of "what" the business does and the technology behind it.

The technical stuff should follow on from the Why and be kept to an absolute minimum.

Imagine a situation where you are talking to a prospective customer or even investor. If you start with why the business was started and why it exists the conversation might go:

The business is passionate about great design/customer service which means our customers don't need to think about xxxx or their efficiency is impacted by zzzzz.

No more is needed at this stage!

Two possible responses – I'm not interested so no business there, OR

That's really interesting and you seem to have recognised a genuine customer needs, so tell me HOW do you do this?

Hooked – you've started a conversation on your terms which you can develop and where the technical stuff just provides the credentials to support your business proposition.

Another approach might be:

Imagine a world where .... is the norm rather than a hope or aspiration.

"That would be a great world, but how could you achieve this?

The conversation has started again.

It is interesting to note that most successful pitches to investors contain very little technical detail. This is partly to protect the idea but primarily it's not needed. The main purpose of the pitch is to generate excitement and few investors have the detailed technical knowledge to make a decision based on the technology at the first pitch. The technical evaluation is carried out as part of the due diligence process which precedes the final decision to invest.

I've been teaching/tutoring/mentoring on strategy for around 30 years and I've found that many of the theories developed are relevant but can never work on their own. Different theories work well in some situations but can be quite misleading in others. How does the entrepreneur work through this jungle of theories and meet the three criteria put forward by Rumelt?

About 20 years ago I developed the model below to try to distil the critical issues into a simple process that can be used to build a strategy – and then keep it under review because the world is constantly changing.

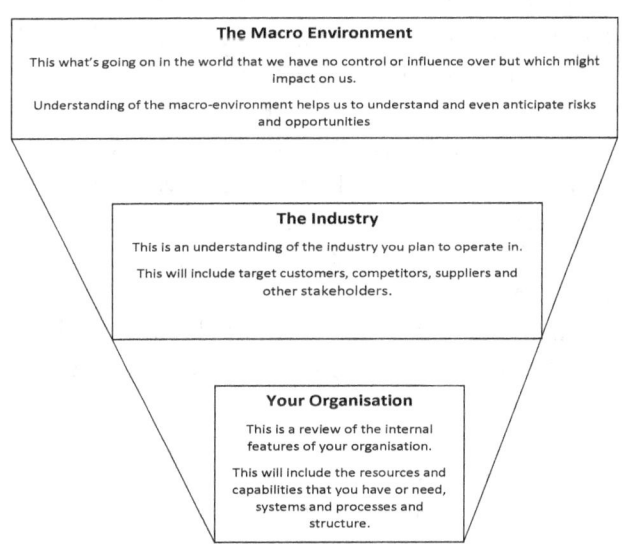

The model attempts to illustrate the very broad and wide assessment of the macro-environment with quite general evidence and data.

At Industry level there is a more focused analysis which generates more detail about the specifics of the industry and homes in on industry statistics.

At Organisation level there is a lot of detail with a lot of focus on the operational detail particularly looking at the way resources interact to create capabilities.

While each level looks independent of the others the reality is that it is a system where each level interacts with each other level.

In a very simple example:

You've identified that the population in Europe is getting older. This might mean that older people may need additional specialised products and services. While many older people live on limited incomes, many have high levels of disposable income due to professional salaries and the certainty of good pensions linked to the mortgage being paid off on a high value property, children no longer dependent etc.

Many of these high income people are also fit and active and looking to explore the world – they have time on their hands and the funds to enjoy themselves. Many might be interested in cultural as well as active leisure time.

You decide that there is a big opportunity for organised holidays/trips with guided walks.

There seems to be a market but what about the industry. Your research shows a number of businesses already offering these types of holidays in different parts of the world. You can see that pricing looks to range from budget to premium depending on a variety of factors such as travel options, group discounts, levels of support from guides, types of accommodation etc.

You work out that different buyers in this industry have different requirements and expectations. Suppliers generally are quite plentiful with plenty of travel options and hotels keen to accommodate groups of mature adults with spending power. There are plenty of potential substitutes as this is based on discretionary spending and can include golf breaks, camper vans etc. Barriers to entry are quite low and industry competition is quite strong but it is a growing market so there is potential to enter the market.

The analysis highlights that some niche segments might be created and you look at combining walking holidays with archaeology activities with a strong initial focus on Greece and Italy – where there is a lot of potential for both activities.

This leads to the organisation structure which needs to provide the resources and capabilities to attract the appropriate target customers and support them during their holiday – and perhaps afterwards.

The business model now evolves to establish suppliers of archaeological sites in Greece and Italy as well as museums and exhibitions that support the cultural activities. There is a need for local guides for the walks and suitable hotels and restaurants to underpin the trips. This is just the basic research and process of developing the capabilities.

Then you can start looking at the profile of your target customers in more detail. Perhaps some cooking and wine tasting activities can be built in as optional extras. Can you provide some guest speakers to talk about the local archaeology and history. How much personalisation can you provide. Singles travelling alone are quite common but the hotels must be able to accommodate at a reasonable cost.

You should see the interconnections between the three levels of the model. But it goes further as now you've built your business model you can go back and fine tune the demographics and social indicators. You can check out all the supplier issues and how your competitors might react. Importantly all of this helps to formulate a pricing structure which is attractive to your target customers but also generates a realistic profit margin.

This is a simple example but don't underestimate the time and effort in developing the initial idea into a realistic business which can work.

Many models often look very static. I like to try to bring them to life. Try drawing the model and the three levels on a large sheet of flipchart paper and then use post it notes to literally throw your ideas at the model. Don't be too structured and keep going until you simply run out of ideas (or energy). Then take a different colour of post its and look at the gaps – things you don't know but think you should, things you know a bit about but think you should know more. Gradually you build up a picture of what the external environment looks like with the risks, threats and opportunities and the resources and capabilities that you have or need. You can even start to timetable the issues – things you need immediately and things that are longer term. This all helps with the financial planning and the implementation plan.

Analysing the Macro-environment

There are a variety of academic frameworks to help develop the analysis. At the macro-environment level it is common to undertake a PESTLE analysis which helps to categorise the main elements. This framework is derived from the original PEST model developed by Fahey and Narayanan[5] which stand for:

Political – What is the political situation in relevant parts of the world?

For example, in the UK the political issues around Brexit are impacting on business between Northern Ireland, the Republic of Ireland, mainland Britain and the rest of Europe.

Tensions between USA and China might disrupt supply chains and are already a source of friction in some industries.

However, forest fires and floods are destroying communities but have created opportunities in flood defence etc.

Economic – Global recession or recovery can have a big impact on many organisations. Issues such as levels of Gross Domestic Product (GDP) and whether it's growing or shrinking and at what rate can help us understand risks and opportunities.

Social – This considers the way society and people behave and changes that may take place as a result. This is often linked to demographic issues such as birth rates, employment and unemployment, poverty etc.

Technological – This is perhaps one of the most dynamic and rapidly changing areas with developments in space travel, satellites, Artificial Intelligence, drug developments, medical treatments – the list just keeps growing.

Legal – This is often overlooked but there is a lot of legislation and regulation to consider which can impact on the organisation. Patents, contract conditions in different countries, employment, environmental, health and safety laws etc.

Environmental – There are lots of issues at global and local level to consider in terms of pollution, climate change etc. This is creating both opportunities and threats. Good white wine is now produced in the UK.

This is only a very simple overview but it is important to consider the macro-environment as a system (Fahey and Narayanan)[4] where each element can impact on any or even all the other elements. For example, a government may decide to reduce Value Added Tax to promote domestic consumption. This increases spending power of consumers creating a social impact which also has an economic impact of reducing the VAT per item purchased but may generate greater tax overall through increased volume consumed. This in turn may have a negative impact on the environment with green groups seeking to change the policy and even pursuing legal action.

There is no judgement in the right or wrongs of any actions just a recognition of the risks and opportunities facing every organisation and the importance of not ignoring the realities.

I'm often asked where do you stop? If you considered everything you would never get past the analysis. There is a judgement to be made which depends on your perspective and the context. I recommend an initial analysis which establishes a framework of information and evidence. Try to keep this up to date and keep monitoring. The three key elements suggested by Rumelt should form the framework.

Publications and news feeds can be useful. There are also lots of organisations that publish relevant useful information. You have to find the sources that suit you.

Some examples:

The Economist is one of my favourites.

The Financial Times, Wall Street Journal and others provide good information with a business focus.

I get a daily news feed to my email from Reuters. There are also technology feeds etc.

Many News services provide good background information.

There are many more but beware of bias. Every publication has some form of bias which presents information in a particular way or style. Be careful not to believe everything and always try to cross check information with alternative sources.

Analysing the Industry

Understanding the way an industry works is critical to your success if you decide to enter a particular industry. Michael Porter[6] is famous for his work as an economist in researching how industries operate and this is reflected in his Five Forces Model.

While it was developed over 40 years ago and has been criticised by some academics and practitioners I believe it is still a useful framework to understand the workings of an industry. The basis of Porter's work is to understand the profit potential or attractiveness of a specific industry by analysing the five forces that influence this attractiveness.

One of the problems cited is that many industries are difficult to define compared to when the model was developed in 1979. How do you define the industry that Amazon operate in? You could argue that they operate in five or six industries – not counting space travel. I tend to agree with Porter that this reflects limitations by the user and we need to be realistic in the way we define the industry and be flexible in the way we apply the model. If it's too broad we get a very general overview that doesn't help in developing the strategy. If we make it too narrow we end up with the same problem as analysing the individual organisation.

Another criticism is that it doesn't work for public sector organisations, NGOs, charities etc. It may not be as clear cut but perhaps the real problem is that these types of organisations are often very inward looking while the model requires a critical and objective assessment of what's going on outside the organisation.

I am happy to develop a discussion on these issues – check out my website (www.changing-odds.com).

Before looking at this in more detail it's important to stress that the analysis is focused at industry level and should not be used to analyse an individual business or organisation. It is a great temptation to try to apply it to a specific organisation and I've tutored many MBA students who have tried this and got into a real mess.

The reason is that the great temptation is simply to list the things the organisation does in each of the five forces. This usually simply becomes a list of what the organisation is good or bad at. This may be useful but it doesn't help to develop a realistic strategy as it just considers the here and now rather than looking at the broader issues impacting on the overall industry.

We handle these organisational aspects at the third level of analysis. This helps to bring all the evidence together into a cohesive strategy that meets Rumelt's three criteria.

The basic model looks like this:

As a generic model it's great as I would argue that every organisation, including the public sector faces these forces. The important issue is that they are different for different industries and contexts. So the first stage is to define the industry that we want to analyse. If we plan to work in more than one industry or where there are overlaps then be prepared to analyse each one.

It's not just about listing the players such as a list of suppliers to the industry but also the bargaining power of each player. For example, an industry which has a few major suppliers who dominate the supply side of the industry can, in many cases, dictate prices which will impact on the ability of the industry to maximise profits.

The same principle applies to the buyers or customers as well as potential entrants. Potential entrants reflects the barriers to entry. An industry which has high entry costs will make the industry attractive to the incumbents but less so for new entrants – unless they have substantial funding available and are willing to take risks.

Threat of substitutes is always quite difficult to assess. My own view is a substitute is a product or service which can divert spending away from the core industry. A substitute may be a new entrant with a disruptive idea.

As with the PESTLE analysis the interaction of the various forces can highlight a range of risks and opportunities and may be a source of ideas for disrupting an existing and apparently stable industry.

One of the best uses of this model is highlighted in Rumelt's[7] description of using it in an MBA tutorial to discuss the potential future of an organisation called Global Crossing. This is a fascinating discussion which is summarised in his book Good Strategy/Bad Strategy. I won't spoil your fun in reading this!

Analysing the Organisation

The third level of analysis helps to bring all the issues into focus. You might find lots of great opportunities with the external analysis of the macro-environment and the industry but is the organisation capable of taking advantage of the opportunities, minimising any associated risks and generating a suitable profit or surplus? It sounds simple but is probably the most complex part of the analysis.

Much of this is based on the work of Jay Barney (1991)[8] and Robert Grant (1991)[9] which essentially recognised that organisations can impact on their success and profitability by the way they utilise their resources to create capabilities. Resources on their own don't add any value but successful organisations co-ordinate and combine these resources to create capabilities which might be able to create a competitive advantage.

As Rumelt has identified many strategies are no more than aspirations. Many strategy workshops focus on "blue sky thinking", "thinking outside the box" and lots of other supposedly inspirational phrases. The reality is that they mean nothing as a strategy until you can turn them into a real and actionable plan and programme of work. To achieve this you must have a clear, objective and realistic assessment of the capabilities that are needed within the organisation to turn the aspirations into reality.

This can be quite challenging and is often not helped by adding more meaningless phrases such as "stretching the envelope".

The analysis must consider not just the current capabilities but also those that will be needed as the organisation grows – often in the face of increased competition and changing markets. This highlights the way the three levels interact.

I've used Amazon in several examples so let's go back to 1996 when Jeff Bezos started the business. Here's a quick summary of the strategic logic:

The original vision was to create the largest online retailer on the planet based on the actual and potential capabilities of the internet. We take all of this for granted now but in 1996 this was quite radical thinking but underpinned by the analysis of the macro-environment.

Why books as a start? The book industry was very stable, very mature and with a number of major incumbents as well as many small players. This made it ripe for disruption. This flowed from analysis of both the macro- environment and the industry.

Books are easy to package and ship and descriptions are clear and coded (the ISBN system). This means the shipping process is simple and returns are low and easy to re-use.

Why Seattle as a base? As a border city there were some tax benefits and Seattle is home to several book publishers. It's also home to Boeing with lots of IT specialists.

Set up a web site, take orders and payments, order the books and collect them in the pick up truck from the publishers, Back to the garage to pack and label them for the customers and down to the post office to post them so they arrive within a very few days.

As the business grows recruit supply chain logistics experts, IT experts and build the systems and processes.

And they keep building…..

This seems to meet Rumelt's three criteria quite effectively even though I've simplified a lot of the detail:

A diagnosis that defines or explains the nature of the challenge. A good diagnosis simplifies the often overwhelming complexity of reality by identifying certain aspects of the situation as critical.

A guiding policy for dealing with the challenge. This is an overall approach chosen to cope with or overcome the obstacles identified in the diagnosis.

A set of coherent actions that are designed to carry out the guiding policy. These are steps that are co-ordinated with one another to work together in accomplishing the guiding policy.

Final Thoughts

While much of this chapter has focused on established businesses it's worth remembering that many of these factors still relate to small or micro enterprises often run by a sole trader or self-employed person.

Personal services such as hairdressers, beauty therapists, physiotherapists, etc can still be impacted by the combination of factors influencing strategy. Problems with supply chains can disrupt the availability of beauty products and equipment. The lesson here is to understand the risks of long supply chains with potential tariffs, delays at ports of entry – all of which are evident in 2021 due to Covid 19, Brexit, USA and China trade disputes and others. These issues will not go away. They will change but they can't be ignored.

Plumbers may rely on copper pipes and fittings and such commodities can become in short supply resulting in price increases and lack of availability. Copper and many other commodities are produced in a wide variety of countries and the so called geopolitics can get quite complicated.

So let's just go back to Rumelt's starting point – "What's going on here?"

This helps us distil our ideas into some simple statements. This is important because many entrepreneurs never get off the ground because they have too many ideas. This may seem a strange problem and counter intuitive when we're being encouraged to be creative and innovative.

I have sat through many pitches and presentations that have never progressed past the initial idea. There is no structure or clear explanation on the commercialisation other than vague aspirations – as highlighted above. This is a natural starting point but how does the entrepreneur progress from the initial idea.

There are many approaches that could be applied. I have a methodology which seems to work for a lot of people.

I'm a fan of mindmapping as well as the use of creative thinking. My "old fashioned" approach is to start with a big plain wall and a box full of post it notes. I know there are software products that can replicate this and I also use a very good mind mapping package[10] which combines brainstorming with the mind mapping and even project planning.

The principles are the same whether on the wall or on the screen. Take a post it note and write down the original idea – not too much detail. A word is too short, a paragraph too long – just a short sentence that encompasses the key idea. Put this in the centre of the wall and then expand the idea with as many post it notes as you can generate – each with a single statement. Don't make judgements or try to organise your thinking at this stage. All you are trying to do is to empty your head of all the random ideas that have been circulating in your brain, often bumping into each other and creating both new ideas and confusion.

This process may take a few hours or a few days. Try not to take too long as there will be plenty of opportunity to expand later. Take a break and then go back to the wall, stand back and look at your idea which has now been turned into a resource that can be developed. You should start to see duplication, overlaps of ideas and some groups of post it notes forming into categories or clusters. You can now start moving the post it notes to create these clusters. As you create these clusters on the wall it will probably trigger new ideas – generate new post it notes and add them where necessary.

When you've generated the clusters, stand back and look at your idea which has now developed into a business model with some structure. Every model will be different but the new structure enables you to understand the issues facing the new business and will help you focus on the categories to develop first and identify those categories that need to be developed later, perhaps when there is an established supply chain or customer base.

Now you have some focus you can start developing the detail for the priority clusters. This is the beginning of a business plan and the pitch – and is where much of the hard work starts. You should have started to identify many areas where you need more information and research.

This approach can also help reduce the bias in your own head that comes with "I have a great idea, it's a guaranteed success". You should incorporate into your post it notes the potential problems, the lack of knowledge, the nagging doubts that you don't want to take over. They may be real – don't bury them, identify them, put them on a post it note and confront them.

Chapter 9 - Avoiding failure – or understanding how to deal with it.

Warm Up Question:
What scares you most about setting up your own business?

In the UK there is a long tradition of considering that failing in a business venture is something to be ashamed of – this gives the idea of being an entrepreneur a bad name. In other countries – notably the USA - failing in a business venture is seen as part of the development process. Getting it right first time is acknowledged as being very difficult.

The reality is probably somewhere in between these two views (and cultures).

I hope by now you are realising that there are many ways to reduce the risk of failure - but there are no absolute guarantees. In this chapter we look at how to recognise the impending problems – it often creeps up on you. If you can spot the signs then you can try to manage the way through it all and if all else fails then at least be in control at the end rather than becoming a victim with all sorts of financial and reputational damage.

You won't know it's happening unless you have the right information – at the right time. If you wait until the end of the year, send all the paperwork to an accountant, wait three months for the accountant to prepare the accounts and then discover you've made a big loss it's not a good start to the recovery. Getting the results usually coincides with contact from the bank concerned with the level of overdraft and asking for the latest accounts.

Another clue that things may not be going well is the constant pressure to pay your bills – even when the business seems to be very busy. There is a term "over trading" which highlights the difference between profits and cash. You may be selling lots but you've given your customers 30 days to pay and many are taking 60 days. Because you're still a new business some of your suppliers require paying immediately on delivery and the rest are strict about payment within 30 days. Gross margin also has an impact – a low gross margin just adds to the cash flow crisis.

Look at the following scenario:

The business has been ticking along with regular monthly sales of £70,000 which is just above break even. Then sales start to take off – great news as profits are rolling in. The bad news is that working capital is soaring and cash is flowing out of the business. The more the business grows the faster it burns cash.

This is a real problem for many businesses – particularly those that are pursuing rapid growth. Unicorns often fall into this category. They need investors with deep pockets and lots of patience. This is not always available to smaller businesses with limited ambitions.

Core data for management control	
Debtor Days	60
Creditor Days	30
Gross Margin%	30%
Inventory (Stock) Days	30

Period	1	2	3	4	5	6
Sales	100,000	120000	150000	170000	200000	230000
Cost of Sales	70000	84000	105000	119000	140000	161000
Gross Profit	30,000	36,000	45,000	51,000	60,000	69,000
Overheads	20000	20000	20000	20000	20000	20000
Net Profit	10,000	16,000	25,000	31,000	40,000	49,000
Cash Flow						
Income	70000	70000	100,000	120,000	150,000	170,000
Expenses						
Inventory Value	70000	84000	105000	119000	140000	161000
Inventory Additions	21000	14000	21000	14000	21000	21000
Overheads	20000	20000	20000	20000	20000	20000
Cost of sales	49000	70000	84000	105000	119000	140000
Opening Balance	10000	-10000	-44000	-69000	-88000	-98000
Period Cash Flow	-20000	-34000	-25000	-19000	-10000	-11000
Closing Balance	-10000	-44000	-69000	-88000	-98000	-109000

Even with investors this business model is not sustainable in the long term and even with low interest rates on debt the charges keep going up. So what do we do?

The first thing is to look at the core data – can we change any of the parameters. Many of these will have been imposed by external stakeholders (suppliers etc) but some can't be changed. We still have to pay staff at the end of each month, rent and taxes have to be paid and some expenses are critical to the performance of the business – web site maintenance, marketing and advertising etc.

Can we get our customers to pay sooner – perhaps with an early payment discount? But don't give too much away! Perhaps the discounts can be linked to contract terms giving longer term assurance of repeat sales. This may provide better planning which links back to suppliers. With greater certainty over sales we might be able to negotiate longer payment terms or faster supplier lead times so that we can reduce inventory levels.

All of these actions (and more) are possible – if we know what the problems are and this means having effective control and management information.

Let's re-jig the numbers – just a bit – and see the impact.

Core data for management control	
Debtor Days	45
Creditor Days	30
Gross Margin%	30%
Inventory (Stock) Days	25

Period	1	2	3	4	5	6
Sales	100,000	120000	150000	170000	200000	230000
Cost of Sales	70000	84000	105000	119000	140000	161000
Gross Profit	30,000	36,000	45,000	51,000	60,000	69,000
Overheads	20000	20000	20000	20000	20000	20000
Net Profit	10,000	16,000	25,000	31,000	40,000	49,000
Cash Flow						
Income	70000	120000	110,000	135,000	160,000	185,000
Expenses						
Inventory Value	70000	70000	87500	99167	116667	134167
Inventory Additions	21000	0	17500	11667	17500	17500
Overheads	20000	20000	20000	20000	20000	20000
Cost of sales	49000	70000	84000	105000	119000	140000
Opening Balance	10000	-10000	20000	8500	6833	10333
Period Cash Flow	-20000	30000	-11500	-1667	3500	7500
Closing Balance	-10000	20000	8500	6833	10333	17833

Don't forget the lessons in Chapter 5 about the Cost/Volume curve. With this growth there may also be opportunities to negotiate better prices from suppliers – which will increase Gross Profit and Margin.

With the information and understanding how to use it you can be pro-active rather than reactive.

The above scenarios show the risks of growing too fast without effective control or understanding of the key principles of managing working capital, the balance sheet and cash flow.

What about the other end of the spectrum – sales are not coming in as expected. Perhaps the business is operating below break even (see Chapter 5). This can be caused by various factors and at different stages of the business development.

If the problems are in the early stages of the start-up then a review of the business model and the background research. Problems in the early stages are often a consequence of poor research and under-estimating the timescale for achieving break even and the consequences for start-up capital and funding. We covered this in Chapters 1 and 6.

Immediate action requires a review of the original business proposition – critically. This is where a mentor can often be a big help. Many people think that asking their accountant (if they have one) is the first step. Many accountants can be very helpful but it's important to remember their primary role is to compile accounts etc – these are historic figures which may not reveal the underlying problems in the business such as customer targeting, pricing policy, contract terms. The important action is that the business owner takes control and is decisive.

Another common problem comes some time after the business has successfully started. The business has grown steadily and the owner/directors decide to start expanding. This can be challenging and risky and many business owners decide to play safe and just keep the business small. This is down to personal choice as well as recognising the limitations in the business in terms of skills, resources and the time and commitment to grow. This is covered in more detail in Chapter 8 on Strategy. The reality is that the early stages involve lots of time and hard work. This might settle down after a period of time and the owner just gets comfortable and doesn't want to go back to the frantic activity of the early days.

A growth strategy often involves investment in additional staff, new equipment, training, additional working capital (stock, debtors etc) and all of this entails risk.

Just to give a simple example of the issues, recruiting a new sales person in a business generating 50% gross margin requires a minimum £100,000 new sales to justify a £50,000 pay package. This ignores all the peripheral costs that will also increase fixed costs (overheads) such as car, expenses staff support etc. This could easily double the sales needed to justify the new position. It's almost certain that the new sales person will need time to build contacts, establish credibility – don't forget these need to be new sales, not just taking over existing sales. This time lag to reach the required performance generates a drag on both profits and cash flow.

So things start to go wrong. Don't ignore the signals – act!

Talk to suppliers about extending payment terms or re-scheduling back payments that are being chased by the suppliers. Suppliers and creditors can often be flexible if given a realistic scenario. Nobody likes nasty surprises. The alternative for the supplier is to pursue and potentially be faced with a bad debt which a can't be recovered.

The same principle applies to all creditors – the bank, loan companies, landlord etc.

To be credible there must be a realistic likelihood that the business can be turned round and so the following should be considered as basics:

If the business is operating at around break even and has a high gross margin (say higher than 55%) then accelerating sales might be a good solution.

Are additional sales available?

Are promotions and discounts needed – check the impact on gross margins.

What are the cost/volume implications – check out Chapter 4 Finance Essentials.

Does the product need a re-vamp, new packaging etc?

If the business is operating at or around break even with a low gross margin (say 25%) then reducing fixed costs is often critical. Increasing sales will have a much smaller impact on profits with a low gross margin than with a high gross margin (see Chapter 5).

Reducing fixed costs may mean selling equipment – which might give a short term boost to cash flow although there may be penalties if under a hire purchase or finance agreement.

Outsourcing parts of the business means they are only paid for when they are linked to sales. This may come at a premium but it should be a serious option.

Permanently reducing staff may be needed – but more work for remaining staff might only be a short term reality before stress and fatigue kicks in.

If the business is well below break even then maybe it's not sustainable and the best option is to consider closure. This can be heart breaking but may eliminate months of stress and hardship if it's unavoidable.

There are a range of processes that can be followed to exit the business. These will vary from country to country but a common theme is that directors have a legal responsibility to ensure that they do not continue to trade if the business is insolvent – it has a negative net asset value on the balance sheet. This can be tolerated if the shareholders, lenders and other key stakeholders are willing to support the negative values and ensure the business continues to receive the funds needed to trade and pay creditors.

Deliberately trading while knowing the business can't pay its bills can be considered fraud with serious implications for the directors. Ignorance is not usually accepted as an excuse. It is the directors who have the responsibility for managing the organization and are therefore accountable.

Now for some of the practical stuff.

If the business is getting into trouble don't just ignore it – the problems won't go away unless you do something.

If you have regular management accounts produced use them to analyse what's going wrong. If you don't have management accounts which are up to date – get them done. You may need to get an accountant to help you. Be honest and open. The accountant can help you get a picture of where you are now – how big are the losses, what have been the trends?

Where are the clues?

Sales volume – both units and total value. How do these compare with your forecasts? If sales volume units is OK then perhaps you're selling below your planned prices, giving discounts etc.

Cost of sales – your original business model should have indicated target Gross Margin. Are you achieving this. If it's too low then you may be paying too much compared to your plan or you may be wasting materials and resources. Wastage can be very critical in many industries, particularly food production, restaurants and bars. How do you find out? Go and check the bins and the bills for waste disposal.

You should check everything but focus on the big items first – these are where the biggest losses can occur and the biggest benefits are gained if you put things right.

These are examples of looking back at the history of how your business is deteriorating.

You should also look forward.

What's the current order book and over what period does it spread?

What are the costings and prices in the order book and does this tally with the historic analysis. If the past tallies with the order book then you need to re-assess the business plan, the feasibility of the business, break even etc (see Chapter 3).

Is there a pipeline of sales enquiries and what's the expected conversion rate into firm orders? This gives you a longer term picture – but it's less certain.

Is a cash flow problem being caused by customers taking longer than expected to pay and/or suppliers demanding early or up front payment. This may be down to negotiation on payment terms – see examples earlier in this chapter.

Take a cold, hard and critical look at all the evidence and information from your analysis. What action is needed to bring the business back on track? Can you scale the business down, such as reducing overheads/fixed costs? This might just be a temporary measure while you try to drive more sales. It's at this stage that a mentor can be really useful – they should ask the tough questions that you may find difficult to ask yourself.

You may decide that the business is not viable in it's current state. This may not be your fault. External factors can change unexpectedly. We had the financial crash of 2008 and now the uncertainty of Covid 19 in 2020 and likely beyond.

If you decide to close the business do it in an orderly and legal fashion. The precise liabilities and costs will depend to a large extent on the way you set up the business – sole trader, partnership, limited company etc. You should understand and check out all the liabilities such as loans, overdrafts, HP agreements, leases and personal guarantees. Limited liability status offers some protection to shareholders but even then you may have provided personal guarantees etc.

Your liabilities may be limited as long as you have not traded negligently, fraudulently or wrongfully.

If you deliberately continue to trade knowing (or you should have known) that you had no chance of trading out of the problem then you might be held liable for losses incurred by creditors in the event of an asset shortfall. It is the directors that are held liable as they have the legal duty to run and manage the company. Remember the "dual personality" we discussed in Chapter 1.

Understanding the principle of solvency which is demonstrated in the balance sheet is critical in this process. If your balance sheet shows negative net asset value than you should either correct it or take steps to close the business. Correcting the negative net asset value involves injecting additional capital, arranging additional financial guarantees and being able to trade out of the problems – but quickly. You should not be continuing to trade without the prospect of rapid (a few weeks) and significant positive changes to the balance sheet. You should now be talking to your account and/or an insolvency professional. Taking appropriate professional advice helps to mitigate risk and blame.

However, remember these are professional people and they need paying for their services even if they are closing down the business.

Finally a real life example:

Some years ago I was approached by a couple who had built up a successful business over a period of 20 years. In the early stages they had agreed an overdraft with their bank and had used their house as security. They then forgot about it as business was good and all seemed fine.

They decided to expand and recruited a sales person to help the owner/MD who had always done the selling and all quotations. The business sold floor products to commercial organisations – a business to business operation usually involving tendering to win work.

The new sales person looked fantastic. New sales rolled in and the installation team was expanded to deal with the additional work. The company did not maintain regular monthly accounts and relied on the accountant that they had used since starting the business to compile annual accounts at year end.

My first phone call explained they had just received the annual accounts which showed a loss of over £50,000 on a turnover of around £1 million. They had never built up significant reserves and the loss put the balance sheet into a negative position – insolvency. The reality is that the problems had probably been creeping up on the business for a few years due, in part, to lack of detailed control.

At our first meeting they confirmed that they had checked back on the jobs sold by the new salesman. The jobs had been won on low prices – too low.

When I arrived for the first meeting they had already taken the first actions. The salesman had been dismissed, the workforce reduced and some vehicles sold. They were working at the limit of their overdraft and the bank wanted some answers and serious action. Their house was at risk.

There was a lot of detailed work done but the main actions taken were:

Critical review of the costing and quotation system with the MD taking over control again. The systems seemed robust but lacked some detailed control and had just been circumvented by the salesman.

There was no time to do a detailed post-mortem on the historic sales – the important issue was the ability to return to profitable trading.

All outstanding quotes, tenders in the pipeline and enquires were reviewed job by job. The MD had to assess if the quotes were realistic. Any which weren't were immediately withdrawn. All the remaining ones were graded both with the likelihood of winning the work and the time frame for award of contract and duration of project. This provided a basic cash flow profile for potential income.

All costs and overheads were reviewed and all unnecessary costs were highlighted for removal.

Combining the contract forecast and estimated gross profits with the revised cost structure created a new break-even position.

The directors were then faced with a clear decision – can they drive the sales over the next 3-6 months based on the quotes, tenders in progress and enquiries to beat break-even by at least 20%. There's nothing scientific about this estimate, it just provides a confidence level.

Having confirmed this was achievable, a cash flow forecast was compiled both for the directors and the bank. This showed a significant increase needed for the overdraft over the next 3-6 months but with significant reductions thereafter.

The bank were approached and given there was significant security still available to secure the overdraft, the increase was approved.

The directors then worked very hard to deliver the results.

Twelve months later the business was back in a healthy profit, the overdraft was eliminated with a healthy positive bank balance. The bank were persuaded to remove the security on the house.

Long term the business continued to grow and prosper and the next generation of the family are now driving a successful business.

Chapter 10 - The Future

Warm up Question:
What are your biggest fears about the future? Are there opportunities to develop?

PREDICTING THE FUTURE????
"Heavier than air flying machines are impossible."
Lord Kelvin
Royal Society President 1895

"Everything that can be invented has been invented."
Charles Duelle
US Office of Patents 1895

"I think there is a world market for maybe five computers."
Thomas Watson
IBM Chairman 1943

"Computers in the future may weigh no more than 1.5 tonnes"
Popular Mechanics magazine 1949

"we don't like their sound, and guitar music is on the way out."
Decca records rejecting The Beatles 1962

"640 K ought to be enough for any one."
Bill Gates 1981

Hindsight is a great thing but even those with intelligence and access to information can get it wrong sometimes. In fairness to Bill Gates, he also predicted a computer on every desk and in every home around 1980.

The world has always been full of uncertainty but perhaps never more so than now. Over the last twenty years we've had the dotcom crash of 2000, rapid growth during the early part of the new century, financial collapse in 2008 with on-going ramifications and now Covid 19. Add to all of this political instability in many parts of the world, regional conflicts, climate change issues, resistance to globalisation, increasing nationalism and real and potential trade wars. Add to this yet more change with developments in technology, moves away from carbon based fuels, space travel as a tourist industry – the list goes on.

How do we cope with the pace of change and the levels of uncertainty. No one has all the answers.

Philip Tetlock has written a book about Supereforecasters[1]. But this approach doesn't eliminate uncertainty and the techniques require some degree of context and framing which helps to create parameters. This can be useful but doesn't help with extremes or radical uncertainty. John Kay (a "realistic" economist) and Mervyn King (ex-Governor of the Bank of England) put forward some relevant and important ideas in Radical Uncertainty[2] which helps us to understand the scale of some of the challenges.

Changing the Odds is being first published in 2021 as the world is still impacted by Covid 19 and much on-going uncertainty. But there are some interesting signs which might form part of your thinking.

Many of the stimulus packages being put forward by most western governments have a strong focus on environmental issues which links well with the increasing concerns over climate change. There is also a big emphasis on upgrading worn out infrastructure – roads, bridges, rail systems etc.

It is impossible to eliminate uncertainty but it is possible to reduce certain types of uncertainty by applying curiosity, relevant research and recognising trends.

There are certain trends that are reasonably predictable such as elements of demographics. Population and age profiles change over time but the process is usually slow and can be predicted in many ways. In so called developed economies population is ageing as a result of various factors – people living longer, couples starting families later etc. These broad trends are likely (but not certain) to continue but with changes in elements of detail which will impact in ways that are less certain. These factors might include increasing levels of obesity and associated increases in type 2 diabetes, pollution in all forms, after effects of Covid 19…….. The list just goes on and the uncertainty flows from not knowing either the individual scale and, importantly, the combined effect of these uncertainties.

Demographics also cover the issues such as education, ideology, social interaction – in simple terms the world continues to evolve and change. The shift in many parts of the world to so called populist governments and attitudes highlights the way that politics and political instability influence the way the world develops and the way political decisions can have a big impact on everyone.

These are just some of the basics. Let's now add in a range of other factors:

Climate change and global warming

Evidence is highlighted in the 2021 cases of high temperatures, forest fires, massive storms and flooding with more and more areas being affected.

Melting glaciers and polar ice caps are increasingly impacting on sea levels.

The Intergovernmental Panel on Climate Change (IPCC) report 6[3] provides important evidence and information to frame the practical implications of climate change.

Pollution of water and air from existing and historic manufacturing, mining and agriculture is an ongoing problem underpinned by the world's demands for growth and the massive sunk costs in established industries.

Ironically moves towards environmental improvements such as electric vehicles are driving demand for metals and minerals such as lithium, cobalt etc – all of which are mined with significant impact on the environment.

Intensive agriculture is causing massive environmental problems

Deforestation (forests are a natural carbon trap) which is often linked to animal production and crops needed to feed a growing global population.

Animals generate methane gas which contributes to global warming.

Fertilizers are full of phosphates and nitrates. Rain washes these into streams and rivers with massive impact on water quality and the fish and other wildlife.

The original phosphates are usually mined which adds more to the environmental impact.

This is an interesting alternative version of the so called circular economy.

Plastics polluting the planet create massive problems that are still potentially under-estimated in terms of long term damage and impact.

There are many safe and valuable uses for plastics but it is the massive growth in the single use plastics which is creating major problems in the oceans, rivers, landfill etc.

The reality of plastic recycling is that even where recycling technology exists virgin raw materials are plentiful and relatively cheap which means that recycling is often not commercially viable – in conventional costing terms.

However it's not all bad news. Let's consider some of the positives:

Research and development for electric vehicles, battery technology and hydrogen fuel cells is accelerating with increasing levels of investment at all levels.

There is increasing political and legal pressure on fossil fuel producers to cut back on extraction and pay realistic charges for the pollution that they create.

There are some interesting developments for re-use of plastics such as

Construction industry and insulation material

Road construction

There are technology developments for water treatment that can reduce/eliminate the traditional use of chemicals to remove pollutants such as metals and phosphates.

Space technology is improving communications globally.

The pandemic has already reduced pollution linked to business travel with the expansion of virtual meetings – which can also significantly reduce costs.

Artificial Intelligence (AI) promises to change the way we all live – but it's still at a very early stage of development.

These are just some of the more obvious examples and the list keeps growing.

This book is not intended to propose evangelical change such as the destruction of capitalism, vegan eating, shutting down major swathes of industry etc. However, the future holds many opportunities for entrepreneurs in re-thinking future options and innovating in many critical areas. Much of this book focuses on traditional ways to test viability, develop market share, generate profits etc. Increasingly society expects more from a business whether an established one or a start-up. Investor expectations are also changing with many starting to actively promote sustainable businesses for the long term rather than a focus on short term returns.

My proposition for the future is to start the thinking around the future options (both positive and negative). Think beyond the "growth at any cost" model which underpins so much of the traditional capitalist system. I'm not suggesting the use of phrases and words that sound good but often have little, if any, practical substance. Think about what a "circular economy" really looks like and how does it impact on industries and individual businesses. Some of the examples above highlight the way a circular economy – one which links different stages of production, usage/consumption and end of life – can have major negative impact on a long term basis.

The long-term view also highlights the use of the word "sustainable". This begs the questions:

Sustainable for whom?

Sustainable over what time period?

How is sustainability measured?

Some argue that sustainability flows from maximising shareholder value.

Is this really a basis for sustainability? John Kay writes about this in his excellent book Obliquity[4].

Does sustainability for the business simply drive greater consumption of natural resources which leads to greater environmental damage?

There are no simple answers to these questions but to Change the Odds the entrepreneur should be considering the opportunities as well as the threats and not ignoring the realities of the world we all live in and the future we pass on to the next generation and beyond.

I hope you can consider all these options in tandem with the suggestions I put forward about creating realistic and achievable strategies.

A good starting point is to develop creative thinking skills to consider alternative ways of achieving your business objectives. Reframing is a great technique for breaking our cycle of thinking in a conventional way.

The world over the last 20 years has faced overall low interest rates which have helped to stimulate demand and consumption. This has been particularly important given the generally low levels of inflation. Even the financial crisis of 2007-8 did little to upset this relative financial stability, albeit with significant support from central banks and government policies.

This book is being first published towards the end of 2021 when most of the world is starting to get back to some form of so-called normality. But just what does normal now look like?

There is real evidence of shortages in many commodities and products. Supply chains are being disrupted as the supply and demand relationships change for a range of reasons. There is talk of increased inflation with the possibility of interest rate rises as the "normal" response. What are the new working patterns going to be? How will these changes impact on both opportunities and threats to the entrepreneur and the start-up business?

What seems certain is there is still a lot of uncertainty to cope with and the ability to reframe our traditional ideas and methods of thinking need to adapt.

When considering any new business venture and the development of the business plan and the pitching for funding a few elements become even more critical than they have been in the past. The reality is that they have always been critical but investors, lenders, suppliers, customers and employees are now even more focused on them.

This focus is on the risks and sensitivities which might impact on the business. Here are a few examples:

- If the business uses debt as part of the capital structure what will be the impact of an increase in interest rates?
- If inflation rises what will be the impact on the cost structure of the business and the buying behaviour of customers?
- If the business is reliant on supplies from the other side of the world what are the risks to the business from disruption, increased shipping costs, non-delivery etc?
- What is the potential impact of environmental charges being imposed through taxation, tariffs etc?

If these, and other issues, are not addressed and incorporated into the business plan then the sustainability of the business must be in question. This will negatively impact the ability of the business to even get started.

Getting things wrong is risk but acknowledging the risks and managing the business to minimise the risks generates confidence both within the organisation and among the key stakeholders.

Ignoring the risks and just blaming "bad luck" if things go wrong is simply stupid!

Chapter 11 - Success and the alternatives...

Warm up Question:
What do you consider the main features of a successful entrepreneur and the way they set up and run the business? It's a key driver for writing this book.

For many years I've been fascinated by the simple reality that some businesses succeed and others fail. Joseph Schumpeter suggested "creative destruction"[1] as a necessary part of the capitalist systems – businesses must fail in order to make way for newer innovations.

However, let's assume there are two businesses with very similar ideas – which one will succeed, will the other fail and what creates the difference?

This is not philosophy but a serious question as to why some businesses succeed, even with apparently weak propositions – while others fail, with strong propositions and great ideas and even funding.

I believe there's a pattern and a range of profiles that help us understand what maximises the success factors. By this stage of the book you've experienced (I hope) many, if not all, of the relevant tools and ideas behind building a business, creating a business plan, finding customers, raising funding etc.

This information is available to everyone – does this mean that everyone succeeds? The statistics suggest that the majority of people reading this book will not succeed. They may not fail outright but they will not achieve the full potential of their ideas and some will fail.

I've done a lot of research and looked at many businesses – success, failures and those in between.

I believe there is a common thread around the behaviour and thinking of the founders that underpins the root of success.

What follows is a mix of my own observations, research and the use of important and useful academic material which is itself the result of extensive research. I've incorporated some real life situations and asked a few business contacts to write their own versions of success and failure. This is not heavy weight academic stuff. I've tried to distil the key elements into clear and easy to understand ideas and suggestions.

This is all about Changing the Odds.

The academic stuff is based on a range of academic sources including:
Chris Argyris
Richard Rumelt (remember the strategy chapter)
Joseph Schumpeter[1]
Edgar Schein
Herbert Simons

Let's be clear, there are no silver bullets but there are some common themes and behaviours which seem to fit with a profile of success.

One of the common themes is the way we think. Let's start with the ideas of Chris Argyris who developed his ideas about thinking and organisational learning as far back as the 1970s. One of his important publications is On

Organizational Learning first published in 1992[2]. It's a big book covering a wide range of issues and topics.

He is constantly asking the same question framed in different ways – what's going on here and this is echoed by the work of Richard Rumelt in the 2010 book Good Strategy/Bad Strategy in how to start thinking strategically. This is our first linkage.

One of the important ideas from Argyris is Double Loop Learning[3].

The common starting point for many management control issues is the idea of a control loop – usually described as single loop learning. Argyris uses the example of a thermostat to explain single loop learning and it's limitations.

The thermostat is programmed to adjust the temperature to a pre-set value by turning the system on and off until the required temperature is achieved. The system continues to use this simple on-off to maintain the required temperature. The system works very effectively for these simple situations. The set temperature (say 22°) is the "governing variable" which in this simple situation is fixed.

But what if the system is capable of asking "why is 22° the correct temperature?". Let's check the ambient temperature and adjust the target. If the outside temperature is 26° should I just shut down the heating system? If it drops to 15° should I adjust to 24° for greater comfort. The "Governing Variables" are being questioned and adjusted depending on a wider range of external factors and even from the individuals who live within the system.

If we apply this simple example to the real-life situations faced by entrepreneurs the governing variables can become quite complex. A key issue for all businesses is the level of uncertainty in the external environment – the world at large, the industry, communities, government policy etc, etc.

A single loop control system would set budgets and actions as relatively fixed governing variables. Many entrepreneurs will justify this as their single minded commitment to the original business vision. While this is a laudable characteristic in many ways, what if the world changes?

The entrepreneur should always be evaluating the governing variables and adjusting actions and assessing the consequences and then adjusting according to the matches and mismatches.

Argyris argues that the double loop approach demonstrates organisational learning. But let's be clear organisations in themselves don't learn. It is the people that learn and this then contributes to the accumulation of learning, understanding and knowledge which is available to the organisation through systems, processes and the discourse between people. There is little point if the entrepreneur doesn't share and disseminate the learning throughout the organisation. If thinking is not shared and replicated across the business then it will create a closed thinking process that discourages challenging ideas and the business looks inwards. This is also covered in Chapter 13 when we look at the way intrapreneurs[4] can impact on an organisation.

This develops our first link to the culture which the entrepreneur starts to develop and the challenges of maintaining a 'positive' culture.

This brings in the work of Edgar Schein[5] who identified three levels of culture:

Artefacts, easy to see but difficult to fully understand.
Espoused values
Underlying beliefs and assumptions

The artefacts can be simple things such as the dress code. A bank may require suits, collar and tie etc to convey an image of solid reliability, traditional values and even trust – all important attributes for a bank. An IT software business may encourage T-shirts, shorts, sandals etc to encourage people to be relaxed, creative and not feel tied to traditional rules and behaviours which might get in the way of creativity and innovation.

If we move to the next level of espoused values – these are the things the organisation sets out as expected behaviours, attitudes etc. If the espoused values are consistent with the artefacts then things are good. If the leaders in an organisation say one thing and do something else then this mismatch can create negative outcomes, uncertainty and inconsistency – all damaging to the organisation. The real problems develop when the entrepreneur does not realise they are being inconsistent in words and deeds – or deliberately disguise things. This can be very damaging and undermines trust and confidence both within the organisation and with external stakeholders such as suppliers, customers, investors etc.

The underlying beliefs are the most difficult to understand and manage. Even if actions and behaviours at the espoused values level are consistent, the underlying beliefs will impact on behaviours. Imagine an organisation that advocates equal rights and opportunities regardless of sex, religion, age etc and the artefacts and espoused values are consistent. Everyone is paid and promoted according to equal opportunities. But does everyone in the organisation really believe in the underlying principles. They can't be forced to agree with gay marriage, policies to allow flexibility for a variety of religious holidays or even smoke breaks and vegan food in the canteen.

There are always likely to be underlying tensions which can emerge and create problems and even conflict.

Consider just a few of the 2020/21 range of issues and the variety of "underlying beliefs":

Consistency in wearing face masks for Covid19 and acceptance of vaccination.

Black Lives Matters and the different interpretations on what is important

Willingness or reluctance to challenge "fake news" when it appeals to our underlying beliefs

This is a major area of complexity and is probably impossible to manage in any systematic way. However, understanding the issues and the tensions and conflicts that are inevitable is a first step in managing (not controlling) the behaviours across all people within the organisation and the aggregate impact that makes up organisational culture.

Schein cites the work of Argyris in understanding the way people behave when they are challenged on the espoused values and underlying beliefs. Challenging these behaviours and thinking is described by Argyris as "frame breaking" and inevitably causes stress, tension and even conflict.

So how do people and organisations learn and progress with all of these problems?

Argyris suggests this is down to how people think and apply this thinking to their behaviour. He describes this as Model 1 and Model 2 thinking as follows:

The governing Values of Model I are[6]:

Achieve the purpose as the actor defines it

Win, do not lose

Suppress negative feelings

Emphasize rationality

Primary Strategies are:

Control environment and task unilaterally
Protect self and others unilaterally
Usually operationalized by:
Unillustrated attributions and evaluations e.g.. "You seem unmotivated"
Advocating courses of action which discourage inquiry e.g.. "Lets not talk about the past, that's over."
Treating ones' own views as obviously correct
Making covert attributions and evaluations
Face-saving moves such as leaving potentially embarrassing facts unstated
Consequences include:
Defensive relationships
Low freedom of choice
Reduced production of valid information
Little public testing of ideas

The significant features of Model II include the ability to call upon good quality data and to make inferences. It looks to include the views and experiences of participants rather than seeking to impose a view upon the situation. Theories should be made explicit and tested, positions should be reasoned and open to exploration by others.

Emphasize common goals and mutual influence.
Encourage open communication, and to publicly test assumptions and beliefs.
Combine advocacy with inquiry[7].

The governing values of Model II include:
Valid information
Free and informed choice
Internal commitment
Strategies include:
Sharing control

Participation in design and implementation of action
Operationalized by:
Attribution and evaluation illustrated with relatively directly observable data
Surfacing conflicting views
Encouraging public testing of evaluations
Consequences should include:
Minimally defensive relationships
High freedom of choice
Increased likelihood of double-loop learning[8]

OK for the theory so far. Let's try to apply this to real life entrepreneur situations.

The research based business model

Great initial idea, developed using various R&D funding streams – which are self-perpetuating. The inventors become reliant on a steady stream of R&D funding – actually finishing something means a change to a production and sales process. This is outside their skill set – and is also a "frame breaking" situation.

Result: Lots of espoused values stated but the underlying beliefs don't change which means no effective action to commercialise even when faced with major large commercial opportunities. Lots of excuses and denial of reality.

The inventors actually have a comfortable lifestyle based on the grant funding but are constantly short of cash due to the timing delays on the funding. They also have to set up a complex project monitoring process just to manage the grant system.

Real life example:

Ten years (minimum) R&D work supported by around £2 million of grant funding. Excellent results from all trials. Several major industries to apply the technology to with significant environmental benefits. No finished product available – but lots of promises between the inventors and various stakeholders.

The real shame is the environment is deprived of a seriously important technology development along with the commercial benefits for both the inventors and their clients.

An example of the wrong approach with poor control

It starts with an innovative idea for the snack food industry – big but very competitive. Two experienced snack food managers plus two interested "friends" with claimed professional skills in business and finance form the start up team.

The business is located in a depressed post-industrial town in the UK attracting a lot of grants and funding to generate jobs and stimulate business activity.

Detailed business plan generated, potential customers identified, equipment schedule developed – substantial grant funding obtained which triggered a bank loan and overdraft to fund working capital. The bank finance was supported by personal guarantees. The plan required a start up of production with 10 employees which would increase as business and volumes increased.

This was classic single loop learning and Model 1 thinking.

The Technical Director purchased the machinery. He thought he could save money by buying second hand equipment – a good strategy but not if the equipment is in poor condition or not suited to the expanding business needs. The MD was the salesman and started using his network of contacts to sell a well designed and specified product with good branding and packaging. Sounds perfect but the governing variables were fixed.

The business went into liquidation within 10 months, why?

The machinery didn't perform as needed and was constantly breaking down. No contingency for repairs and maintenance so the Technical Director was often seen on his back under a machine fixing it. Good for the multi-tasking but 10 operators were standing watching on full pay. Not good for productivity, output, cash flow and profits.

Shortages in production meant customers were not getting reliable deliveries and the MD didn't want to add to the problems so slowed down on sales and spent more and more time in his office.

The company had weak financial controls and failed to give the bank up to date and reliable figures and even the static budget data had errors. This is not good for maintaining trust and confidence.

Customers started to get nervous about placing large orders due to lack of trust and confidence in reliable delivery.

Suppliers were increasingly being paid late – again a problem for building trust and confidence

The company never got to break even (see Chapter 5).

Underpinning all of this was a classic Model 1 thinking action by the directors. We've worked hard to start the business, raised a lot of money, created jobs – so we deserve to be rewarded. Significant salaries were paid to the directors from the moment the funding hit the bank. Worst of all a week after start up four top of the range brand new executive cars appeared in the car park. Leased but still a long term fixed cost draining cash flow.

Time to reflect as an entrepreneur – what would you do differently? The founders of both businesses both started to recognise the problems but failed to take effective action to create solutions that worked.

Let's consider alternative thinking – Model 2

A good approach from a false start (Shai)

I came across Shai at an early boootcamp at Manchester Metropolitan University. He has a strong technology background and was setting up an app based business. He has returned to bootcamp as one of our inspirational speakers. The simplified story in his own words:

The first business idea was developed without talking to potential customers – a fear of people stealing the idea.

Result – significant under-performance, the app just didn't meet customer expectations because these had not been fully researched.

Next time the app was developed in discussions with potential customers – what features are important, what will you use it for etc?

Result – real success.

Key learning points:
Talk to your potential customers.
Listen to them and don't be arrogant and ignore them.
Act and adapt on what you learn.
Keep learning by talking to people.

The catalyst for success is effective action and the ability/willingness to adapt.

This links the good strategy of Rumelt with the Theory in use of Argyris.

Pulling this together the entrepreneur at most risk of failure is:

Convinced they are right about all the fundamental issues.

They have all the data they need as this just reinforces their core beliefs

Any other data is just a distraction and therefore is discounted/rejected

They discourage any challenges to their thinking which in turn suppresses healthy discussion

They support weak arguments with vague statements such as "Trust me I know it's right" or "you don't understand the problem" etc.

Even when confronted with alternative ideas they are rejected as being irrelevant or not accurate/well founded – regardless of the evidence.

Ready to blame others if things start to go wrong – it's never "my" fault.

The entrepreneur at least risk is always:
Creating inclusive discussion platforms
Sharing ideas and encouraging others to do the same
Willing to admit to limitations and mistakes
Keen to accept advice and help particularly in investigating new ideas and opportunities.

These are not perfect scenarios and you might be thinking of some paradoxes. Single minded determination is often cited as a great entrepreneurial strength. This is true but not when it ignores reality, changes in the external environment or changes in customer needs.

It's easy to assume that the research driven business is constantly looking for new ideas – this is the core purpose for research. However, most researchers are experts in a particular field of technology or knowledge. This can actually drive Model 1 thinking to extremes as anything outside this detailed sphere of understanding is not fully understood and is therefore at risk of rejection or at least being parked. This can be a problem caused by "experts".

Argyris develops this further in Chapter 4 of On Organizational Learning[9] which was reprinted in an article for Harvard Business Review entitled "Teaching smart people how to learn"[10].

This article highlights how "smart" people (consultants and senior managers) do not handle personal challenges or criticism well. This creates a defensive block which means that problems don't get solved – they get attributed to other people, such as another department, the customer etc.

Argyris describes it as:

"Put simply, because many professionals are almost always successful at what they do, they never experience failure. And because they have rarely failed, they have never learned how to learn from failure. So, whenever their single loop learning strategies go wrong, they become defensive, screen out criticism, and put the "blame" on anyone and everyone but themselves. In short, their ability to learn shuts down precisely at the moment they need it most."[10]

The approach to good research – what's going on here, as Rumelt describes it – can be broken down into three key areas:

The first area is fundamental research into new areas of science, technology, engineering, psychology etc which moves human knowledge forward. Many of the ideas may create opportunities for patents which provide an effective monopoly for the inventors to exploit the ideas for a period of 20 years. However, many of these ideas are created in a vacuum where there is no realistic commercialisation plan. There are also major issues about "scaling up" from a lab-based idea at test tube level to large scale production/manufacturing along with marketing and launch logistics.

This is where many start-ups need substantial funding even when they have generated grant funding for the research.

Just a basic patent filing for the UK can cost £10,000 with no guarantees that it will provide the monopoly that generates large sales and premium profits.

Many of such start-ups sell out to a major company with the resources to support the "scale up" process.

Be aware that early-stage valuations may not meet the founder's expectations as the acquirer/investor is still faced with significant risks and costs.

The second key area is Generic Market Research which identifies and correlates publicly available material to provide a general background which may support the initial thinking that drives the Fundamental Research but is also important when evaluating a disruptive business model, perceived gaps in the market place etc. This research is necessary but too often it is simply a compilation of Google (or similar) searches which do no more than provide a simple view of a market or industry. A common framework used in the type of research is PEST or PESTLE analysis which looks at the overarching issues around the political and economic climate, social/cultural issues along with technological, legal and environmental considerations. An important feature is that the organisation has no control or influence over these issues – but they have the potential to have a major impact. The original thinking for this type of analysis was developed by Fahey and Naraynan[11] who described this as the macro-environment which worked as a system where each element interacted with all the other elements creating a complex picture. You can find more detail on this in Chapter 8 – Developing a Strategy.

The third key area is Focused Research which looks at the specific issues which are critical to the organisation and how it develops a commercial plan with sustainability. The organisation has a degree of influence and even control over the issues identified. It is this level of research which is often very weak in many start-up businesses and yet it is critical in the way the business is set up and structured.

It helps to understand the segmentation and 'customer persona' (Chapter 4) which helps with targeting and designing the ways of communicating with the target customers/consumers.

It helps to create focus for the start-up which is critical, particularly in the early stages where there are major risks of trying to attack too many targets which can create confusion among potential customers about what the organisation is trying to sell.

Combining the Generic and Focused research helps to create a credible business model where key characteristics of the market, competitors and customers can be assessed so that a realistic, coherent and credible strategy for implementation can be developed.

However, remember the earlier work from Argyris with double loop learning, Rumelt with "what's going on here?" and Schein with espoused beliefs and underlying assumptions. Once you start the file is always open – you have to keep everything under review.

The objective is to anticipate the impact of changes in the external environment and use this insight to stay ahead of the competition. This may also require updates to the fundamental research to pursue specific new ideas and innovations.

This chapter has covered a wide range of issues some of which are quite complex. I hope the message is clear that just having a good idea or a ground breaking technology is no guarantee of success. Indeed, often this starting point can jeopardise success if the entrepreneur is not adaptive and is able and willing to modify their thinking processes.

On the following page reflect on your answer to the Introductory Question and make notes on how your own thinking process may have changed as a result of reading this chapter – and earlier chapters.

Chapter 12 - Types of Entrepreneur – and possible implications

Warm-Up Questions:
How do you see yourself as an entrepreneur? Why do you want to become an entrepreneur?
What is your overall goal – not just the financial ones?

If you Google this "Types of Entrepreneurs" you will get a wide range of versions and interpretations. Some are helpful, others are less so.

This chapter is focused on trying to explain the different types of entrepreneur based on my own observations as well as some research and discussions with some of the people that I have bounced off in their entrepreneurial journey. Some of these have been brilliantly successful while others have failed – with everything in between.

The focus is on entrepreneurs who are looking to build a scalable business rather than those who might be developing a hobby into a lifestyle business. However, some lifestyle businesses can develop into growth businesses.

Even the word entrepreneur can create misconceptions, and some have tried to add additional description such as an agricultural entrepreneur, small scale entrepreneur and even intrapreneur. I will try to add value to this discussion in an effort to help people understand the driving forces that need to exist, be developed, nurtured and possibly even be rejected. And let's not forget the unicorns.

I've always been fascinated by the motivation behind the entrepreneur. If we agree that starting and/or building a business requires risk taking and a willingness to step into an environment that might be strange – even if you are experienced in an industry, you are still creating a new context for the way you engage with this familiar territory. You may be trying to disrupt an established industry – again, you are changing the context which can bring uncertainty and risk.

I have tried to think of the types of entrepreneurs as a spectrum of features. It is not a linear spectrum and is even a 3-dimensional model with overlapping items.

What do each of these types of entrepreneurs need to help them change the odds?

Before we start let's be clear that this is not a precise science. The categories themselves are quite subjective and based on observation, anecdote and informal discussions. There are lots of overlaps. For example, an inheritor and an inventor may get together, MBO and MBI may combine, the pauper may meet an inheritor at the bottom of a lift with the best elevator pitch on the planet……

The same applies to the suggested ways of structuring and helping the entrepreneur succeed regardless of the starting point.

The Pauper or Zero Entrepreneur
No start up capital
No assets for security
No credit rating
But
Lots of ambition
Lots of Drive and commitment

Let's start at the zero end (pauper) where the entrepreneur has an idea and vision but has no resources. This might be a recent graduate, someone who is long term unemployed, someone wanting to progress from the gig economy…..

There are some critical characteristics:

No financial resources to call on.

No assets to use as security.

Probably a lack of specific and tangible experience for the potential business but this is not always the case.

Not many people are willing to listen and provide practical support due to a lack of (apparent) credibility as a result of the above.

This is a lonely starting place with little scope of raising finance or even attracting the first customer and sale.

However, a different view is that this is quite a low risk for the entrepreneur as there is little to lose except time and effort.

This provides the clue for a possible way to proceed:

There may be limited funding from government schemes to stimulate employment, start-ups etc. This depends a lot on the country and even the region.

Start small and keep re-cycling any generated funds/income.

Beg and borrow stuff from friends, relatives etc – but don't over-promise on returns

Convince customers, suppliers etc of your total commitment and trustworthiness

Don't be afraid to generate income from part-time jobs just to keep paying the bills (and feeding yourself). Despite the bad publicity this is where the gig economy may be useful.

This is where creativity and imagination are critical and developing these skills will be a genuine asset to the business.

Frustrated Staff

Lots of experience and knowledge.

Possibly limited in scope of experience beyond the current job which is driving the frustration.

Feels held back in current employment.

Sees opportunities but needs to frame them in a realistic structure.

Might be able to run a business while still drawing a salary

But

Needs to be careful about employment contract issues.

Perhaps the big obstacle to overcome is mindset. A good friend whose grandfather built a very large engineering business stated that managers don't make entrepreneurs. I'm not fully convinced by this but I do agree that the thinking and actions of a manager are often (usually) different to those of an entrepreneur.

Most managers are paid to maintain stability and meet agreed performance targets. Entrepreneurs seek to disrupt and change the status quo. However, sometimes this can be achieved by copying successful business models – and just doing it better. The challenge is working out what "better" means in practical terms and how does it meet customer expectations.

This takes us back to the creativity and imagination critical for the last group.

So the Frustrated Staff Entrepreneur needs:

A high degree of curiosity.

An ability to shake off any "strategic myopia" as described by Richard Rumelt1.

People who can provide a different context to the problem solving. This might be a mentor.

These people may have different ideas – possibly from the same industry. Context is important.

The proposed business may be in the same industry or in something related or even completely different. Research is critical in order to define the product/service offering in a clear and focused way.

An Angel investor may provide both funding and the mentor capability which is critical to building a team.

Inventor

Perhaps a serial inventor who just likes developing new ideas.

Potential for early stage grant funding if the technology is suitable.

Often a strong academic background.

Possible on-going links with university.

Possible issues over shared IP which may cause problems.

The inventor is often (but not always) linked to an academic background of research. Even without this there is an underlying curiosity with the inventor which seeks to solve a problem or problems. This may be driven from a personal dissatisfaction with a current state of affairs or a vision of a better world – and any variation between these positions.

There is a characteristic about many inventors – isolation.

While they may work in teams in the academic world they are often concerned (even obsessed) with secrecy and the fear that someone may steal their idea. While this may be a valid concern it also highlights a real challenge for the inventor as a successful entrepreneur.

How do you test the validity or application of the invention?

The inventor working in an academic institution is likely to be working under a contract that entitles the university to "own" any IP developed during the normal course of work. There are many academics who are happy with this and pursue a great career in research with publication of papers, conferences and academic recognition as the rewards.

However, if the academic wants to become an entrepreneur based on the research undertaken during the day job then it will be necessary in most situations to get agreement from the employing institution. Most employment contracts in this situation are quite clear and explicit. The university may insist on being part of the invention exploitation. This may not be a problem. The university can provide on-going support, research and development facilities and even credibility. Many universities recognise the positive aspects of this type of collaboration and provide facilities to set up "spin out" businesses to help the commercialisation.

It's important that both the inventor and the university recognise the pitfalls of not getting the balance right. It is common for this type of business to attract funding at an early stage – seed capital, and then get further stages of funding as the invention approaches full commercialisation. The opportunities for funding can be negatively impacted if either side have unrealistic expectations on the valuation at each stage and also the split in the equity.

Many good inventions have failed to get the necessary funding traction because of unrealistic expectations at this stage of the funding process.

The other challenge facing the inventor is just when to stay "stop" – the invention is complete. Moving beyond the idea and invention stage is like stepping off a cliff to many inventors as they have no idea or experience as to what happens next. This links back to the isolation problem. It's at this stage they need resources to progress from invention to prototype, to full working model, to commercialisation.

These phases are about understanding customer, costing and pricing, supply chains, employment issues, IP and licensing agreements. Help is needed otherwise the inventor just keeps doing what they know and do best – inventing. This translates into constant tweaks and updates. When asked by friends and family how the "invention" is going the answer is often the same – "it's going really well, it's nearly finished but just checking out a few things". What is missing is the crucial statement of a deadline or a completion date.

How does this translate into practice and what are the solutions? There is nothing wrong with the inventor continuing to invent, but at what stage do they step off the cliff? It's important to have an independent person to assess the invention at each stage and to suggest when the invention has got to a marketable stage. Bear in mind this is also likely to include prototyping, trials etc. These are necessary stages leading up to launch but are more related to the engineering aspects – how is it produced – as well as all the commercial and logistics issued highlighted above.

The inventor needs to accept closure at this crucial stage of the development and enable the invention as it stands to be assessed and "signed off" to progress to the next stage.

Instead of seeing this as the end of the invention this should be seen as a release for the inventor. The release enables the inventor to use the closure as a platform for future versions and enhancements. This is critical to building a sustainable business.

Reflect on how many great products, software packages, apps and even business models expand and gain traction by having a portfolio of new versions and enhancements. Each one capable of attracting new customers and gaining repeat sales from existing ones.

Consider the updated versions of Apple phones, operating systems and even the connectors. Dyson has taken the core idea of vortex technology and used in a wide range of applications with ever increasing patent and design implications.

To achieve sustainability the inventor and entrepreneur must not starve this future stream of business of investment and this must be factored into any funding structure.

Management Buy Out/Management Buy In (MBO/MBI)

Often triggered by the retirement of the founder or serious under-performance by management team.

Can also be triggered by a divestment from a larger group.

The MBI element may be from the Successful CEO category.

The MBO benefits from inside information on the business.

But beware of "myopia".

A combined MBO/MBI may provide the best of both worlds but the teams must be comfortable with each other.

As an example you work for small to medium business founded by an entrepreneur 30 years ago who has gone through all the challenges and stresses of starting and growing a business. The owner wants to retire and capitalise on the value of the business which has developed and relax a bit.

Or you are the General Manager of a mid sized business which is part of a large group. The large group carries out one of its regular "strategic reviews" and decides that the business that you manage is no longer part of the long term future of the group – not core.

Both of these scenarios provide an opportunity for the manager to become an entrepreneur. There are two issues:

The existing owner wants paying a realistic price for the business.

The business is a going concern with established customers, supplies, processes and systems, trained staff, logistics – in fact a fully functioning business.

There is another factor – as the manager you know everything about the business and hopefully have a view of the future potential under "new management".

It is common for many of these businesses to have "plateaued" due to owner fatigue or a lack of strategic vision. Indeed, why would anyone want to sell a "rising star"? Can you re-inject vigour and vision into the business – based on objective research and assessment rather than just wishful thinking?

The factors that need immediate consideration include:

The quality of the rest of the management team.

The likely value placed on the business by the owners.

How they want/need to be paid.

Your access to potential sources of funding.

Realistic assessment of future growth potential.

Realistic assessment of the risks – competitors, changes in market conditions, product life cycles.

This is not an exhaustive list but provides the starting point for developing the business plan which is necessary to initially assess whether you want to proceed with an MBO and, assuming this is confirmed, the likely structure of any deal. You are now moving from manager to entrepreneur.

Successful CEO (and other senior managers)

The Maslow Syndrome[1]:

This is often represented as a pyramid starting at the base of the pyramid with basic safety and security and progressing through the following levels:

Level 1 (Base)

Physiological – just meeting the basic needs of survival

Level 2

Safety – building family and community links and structures

Level 3

Love and belonging - reinforcing family values and friendships.

Level 4

Esteem – self esteem, building the respect of others

Level 5

Self-actualisation – building creativity, spontaneity, problem solving, lack of prejudice etc.

The successful CEO (or similar) reaches the top of the pyramid (Level 5) and then puts it all at risk by walking away from stability and security.

They have worked hard to reach the top of an organisation as an employee.

This is not good enough, wants to:
· control own destiny
· Find new challenges
· Take risks and even thrills

So you've made it after years of working hard, getting qualified, the MBA from a prestigious business school and years of working up the corporate ladder. The lifestyle is comfortable with large house, a holiday cottage in a nice part of the world, top of the range car, big pension pot and children at a good private school. What could be better?

But you're not really happy. Where are the new challenges? Meeting shareholder expectations is proving harder than you thought and you can't ever really say what you're thinking – it might be mis-interpreted. Perhaps you think that the shareholder needs are too short term.

One solution is to walk away and start something new, something that is yours. This is unlikely to be a spur of the moment decision. The ideas have probably been forming for some time – even years. There might be a trigger event but you resign.

How you become an entrepreneur will vary depending on a number of factors:

If you plan to start up in the same industry/business as your ex-employer there may be restrictive covenants preventing you from doing what you want. These are usually time limited so you may have to sit it out for, say, 12 months.

If you are starting something completely new then these restrictions may not apply but you have the lead time to start from scratch, building a team, finalising the product/service offering.

Funding will always be an issue but this is when your credibility, track record and network can come into play. You need to exploit every contacts, call in every favour – but stay legal.

If it's a new idea this may involve an inventor so remember the inventor characteristics highlighted above. You will be the manager that drives the progress and provides the commercial reality. You need to control things but not stifle the creativity of the inventor – it is this that generates the sustainability.

A few final thoughts that have impacted on some entrepreneurs in this category. You are a corporate person who is used to having a support team, to organise your diary, present you with reports and management data. This is unlikely to be available in the short term. Even if you do a Management Buy In it is unlikely that your target will have the level of systems and infrastructure that you are used to.

If you link up with an inventor there is real risk of a culture and thinking clash. The inventor is used to just doing things without seeking approval. You may be seen as a stifling influence seeking to control everything and having different ideas about acceptable performance, financial returns – in fact almost everything. This is not impossible but it needs a lot of trust and flexibility – on both sides.

An example is Mobileye[2] which is not a well known company but was started around 1999 by two friends with different backgrounds. Amnon Shashua was a professor at Hebrew University in Jerusalem and Ziv Aviram was an entrepreneur and business person. They had a shared vision about autonomous cars and how to develop the technology and commercialise it. The story is fascinating but the key parts are that they built up a business based on the technical genius of Amnon and the financial and commercial genius of Ziv. "Genius" is the way they describe each other. After initial funding rounds they floated on the NYSE in 2014 having just published their first profits in 2013. The initial valuation at floatation was $5.3 billion which quickly climbed to $11 billion.

There are lots of factors driving this success but a critical element was the absolute trust between the two founders and their confidence in each other. Amnon handled all the technical development while Ziv handled all the financial and commercial issues. The overall strategy was a shared vision that they developed and built together.

In 2017 the company was acquired by Intel for $15 billion.

The Inheritor

- Brought up and educated in a "privileged " environment.
- High expectations from family and friends.
- But needs peer recognition and approval from founder which may be both explicit and tacit.
- Has to overcome (or deal with) "silver spoon" syndrome3.
- Has a great start but also lots to lose.
- Scope may be limited by "protective" covenants from founder.
- Often surrounded by "yes" people often hanging onto the coat tails but perhaps not really committed.

This includes the person whose parent or relative started a business or even inherited a family concern and built it into a large business with lots of assets, resources, financial stability, loyal staff and solid lenders.

At first sight this is the "silver spoon" thinking – what could be easier? Perhaps the previous generation has chosen to retire or even died. The reality is that this is probably a more difficult job than any other.

Why?

There is so much to lose. It may seem easy but the new boss has not had the insights and experience of the founder even if they have worked together in the business. Again, it's a new context which needs a re-think on the way forward. If the previous generation has retired it might be that there are issues that they may not feel comfortable with. This is increasingly an issue as businesses have to deal with digital technology, cyber security, environmental issues and artificial intelligence (and a wide range of others).

Often the inheritor entrepreneur is faced with building a new team while maintaining the day to day operations of the on-going business. This is a challenging job at the best of times but the departure of the "old boss" can (does) create lots of uncertainty and this can lead to stress and even conflict. Some of the best staff may simply leave because they can get another job easily. It's important for the new boss to have a clear vision and strategy and be able to communicate this quickly and effectively to all the staff. But be careful of the meaningless strategy statements as described in Chapter 8 Strategy. It's also important to communicate with customers, suppliers and other key stakeholders – continuity is important to maintain cash flow. Ironically this is most important if big changes are planned in the future.

Inheritors may also seek new business opportunities and this is when they will interact with inventors, MBOs and even create a Management Buy In. Combining MBO with MBI can create a very solid structure which benefits from a strong management team, funding and continuity of business.

There may also be opportunities to build new businesses by using the Intrapreneur approach – see chapter 14.

Equity Issues

I have a simple philosophy about equity – keep hold of it and don't give it away. The reasoning is simple:

In the early stages it's not worth much (if anything) so you are likely to give away too much.

Once the business is proven the value of equity can increase dramatically based on confidence in future trading. This raises the risk of letting it go too cheaply or at the wrong timing.

Timing can be critical.

But how do you build a team from scratch – particularly if you have no funds for the business? How do you fill a resource gap (for example, a software engineer critical to the business model)?

How do you know the person(s) you are talking to are "right" for the business? A friend or relative may be nice to work with but relationships change as soon as there is financial reward, shares, employment contracts, shareholder agreements etc to deal with.

I have helped a number of management buy-outs over the years. The scenario is usually the same:

Founder and shareholder wants to retire and realise the value of the business. The simplest option is to sell to the management team – they know the business, the founder (hopefully) trusts them and they have access to all the relevant information about the business which should make raising appropriate finance easier.

There is often a single key person (perhaps two) who will drive the MBO.

There is then a team of skilled and experienced managers – the term "manager" is very relevant in this context. They are used to a regular salary, reliable employment, good benefits and a steady and predictable work pattern.

The lead manager has to question themselves about becoming an entrepreneur:

Do I want to take responsibility for the business at every level possibly using personal assets as security?

How does my family feel about the risks and the opportunities?

Am I willing to potentially sacrifice personal time and space to make it work – and will my family support this disruption?

Having checked all this out the lead manager then needs to ensure that all the potential MBO team can answer the same questions. But then there's the final test I challenge the team with:

We're all on a cruise ship which sinks in the middle of the ocean.

We may be adrift in a life boat with limited water and food (resources) for a long time with no guarantee of rescue.

Are the people in the boat with me the ones I would choose if given the opportunity or would I prefer to have the stoker from the engine room, the navigator from the bridge.....

The key point here is that the business after the MBO will be different from the business prior to the MBO. There are new opportunities, the chance for a new strategy and direction, funding and control will be different, and even suppliers and customers will regard the business differently. And don't forget the employees.

This is not all negative and there can be some major positive factors such as a revitalised business.

What is important is the lead manager must keep control (hands on the tiller in the lifeboat) and take nothing for granted. Remember the Model 2 thinking from Chapter 11.

All of the issues discussed here are based on a traditional view which is underpinned by the way that tangible assets (physical things) are associated with the balance sheet valuation for a business dealing in physical products.

More and more businesses are based on intangible assets such as brand valuation, intellectual property, trade secrets, know how. These are often producing and selling software products, apps and consultancy services. The value of staff in these businesses becomes part of the value and are critical to the development and sustainability of the businesses. Consider relatively mature companies such Microsoft, Amazon and Apple and newer businesses such as AirBnB.

Using equity as an early reward can attract in the high calibre and talented staff that can drive the growth and profitability of the business. Attracting such staff can also be a critical factor in investor funding – they want growth, profits and as little risk as possible. The business can benefit from having the staff it needs without necessarily paying the market rate for salary – the rewards are deferred.

Sounds good but beware of some of the risks:

Staff retained in this way should have an exclusive agreement with your company otherwise they might peddle their skills to other businesses, even competitors.

If they are as good as you hope and expect they are attractive to a wide range of potential employers and other start-ups.

Be reasonable, if you're not paying them much then they still need to eat and live. A second job can be a necessary part of the process.

Trust is a major factor between everyone.

The type (class) of shares used can be quite critical. Try to match the class of share to the needs of both the company and the individual. Starting with non-voting shares may demonstrate commitment with an agreement to provide more "strategic" shares as the relationship and the business viability develops.

Many of these relationships are used to drive investments which might start with seed capital and develop into a full scale private equity investor (see Chapter 6 on Funding). The implications need to be understood as the original shareholders will all face dilution of their shareholding at each round of investment. This can cause resentment and even conflict which may create blockages for the investment for rapid growth.

The equity issues are handled in more detail in Chapter 6 on Funding.

Social Entrepreneurs

The focus so far has been on commercial entrepreneurs. There are also those who are often labelled social entrepreneurs. This term covers a wide range of people and organisations and is often motivated by a sense of social injustice, unfairness and exploitation of the less fortunate.

There are some great social entrepreneurs who I have worked with over the years. There are some common characteristics which underpin their effectiveness, sustainability and success.

Focus on being good at a few things rather than solving the problems of the universe.

Be realistic about the availability of resources and how best to utilise them,

It is unfair and unwise to set up an organisation promising many things, raising expectations and then letting the people down that were the target for the help.

Social enterprises are sometimes called Not for Profit (NFP) organisations. This creates misconceptions. If you don't make a surplus (profit) then you will not build up reserves and so you rely on regular income, grant aid etc to keep operating. This is a high risk strategy and is behind many failures.

Having a structure that suits the purpose of the organisation is critical. This may mean having several non-executive directors who are well connected to build confidence and credibility. This can help with funding, grants etc as well as promoting good governance.

I hope that having read this chapter you will realise that it is very difficult to neatly position any entrepreneur in a fixed category. There are many opportunities for overlap and blending of characteristics depending on the unique circumstances of every business opportunity.

It's useful at this stage to go back to your answers to the warm-up questions. Have you changed your thinking with these additional insights?

I hope you can now start pulling together the strands of your business which reflects a realistic structure and a business model that makes sense and can provide a platform for a sustainable business.

The following page is blank so you can make notes about any thoughts you have about being an entrepreneur. How has your thinking changed since thinking about the question at the start of this chapter? How will this help your entrepreneurial journey?

Chapter 13 - The Intrapreneur

Warm up Question:
What is an intrapreneur and why might it be relevant to you – or not?

Oxford Dictionary Definition:

A manager within a company who promotes innovative product development and marketing.
With a suggested example as:
'Rather, as happens in a franchise where an individual buys into a successful business concept, an intrapreneur benefits through being able to trade on the reputation of the parent without having to start afresh.'

I have a problem with the word Intrapreneur which seems to create a label for something that already exists – or should exist in every organisation. I also have a problem with the definition – why just a manager? Why not anyone in the organisation?

If we start with the basic starting point for any entrepreneur – they have an idea. Many of these ideas are related to their background, education, qualifications and, importantly, their work experience.

The danger of using a simple word that is fashionable is that it is open to many interpretations. The following overview may be a bit controversial but perhaps it will stimulate some realistic thinking and action on an important business issue.

I want to start by looking at the organisation not as a formal structure of departments, reporting lines, chains of command etc, but as a social network of people with ideas working within the formal structure which might be represented in a simple way as:

The Organisation
Structure and formal chains of command
Departments
Fulfilling functional responsibilities and maintaining the day-to-day operations
Interest Groups
Informal (and formal) groups that have similar or common interests.

These may be project teams or small groups that "hang out" together and discuss anything from fashion, football or technology – in fact anything.

These groups are "self- managing" even when project teams have reporting responsibilities.
Individuals
While each employee and sub-contractor will have a contract of employment or services this does not reflect their full potential or special interests and skills.

This covers everyone from the CEO to the lowest paid junior in the organisation.

The Board of Directors in an organisation usually sees itself as the driver of all new ideas with the power to decide on strategy and the direction the business will take. Many of these Directors have progressed from within the organisation and have accumulated a lot of knowledge and experience –

about the way the organisation has worked in the past. Indeed, many of them will have taken the credit for innovations and new ideas which has helped their progression.

All of this knowledge and expertise at board level comes with a big risk. Having reached the top of the tree there is a great temptation to defend the past actions and dismiss new ideas as "not what we do here". This can be a very effective strategy in maximising the utilisation of existing assets and resources but can be very dangerous in turbulent markets and industries.

Richard Pascale[1] highlighted many of the problems in his article Surfing the Edge of Chaos. He highlights that stability and predictability are often the death of an organisation. The death may not be quick and may be a long lingering decline. This is also highlighted in a model used in many strategy courses – The Strategic Drift model[2]:

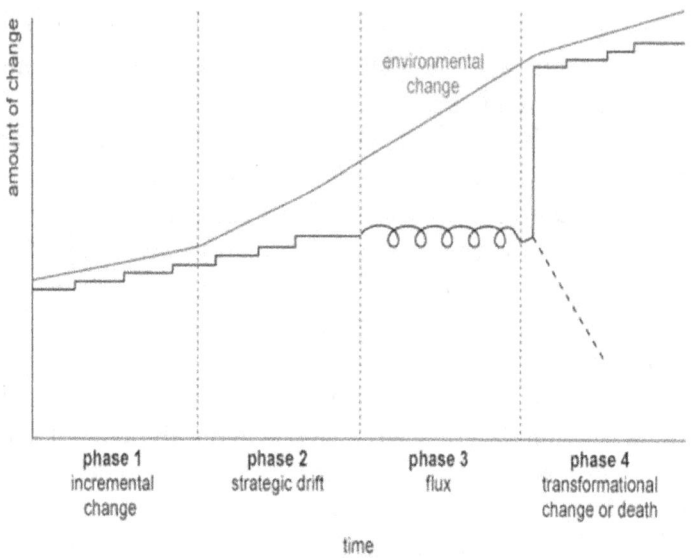

This model shows the various stages of drift as the organisation drifts away from the reality of the external environment in which it operates. The initial response is often small incremental changes which are reactive rather than proactive – anticipating the need for change.

These incremental changes continue as the strategic drift becomes more pronounced and is often followed by a state of flux where lots of things are tried but they continue to be reactions rather than a well thought out strategy. The final phase reflects an organisation that has lived in isolation from the real world and is faced with transformational change or death. These are sometimes called "bet the farm" strategies.

Rumelt develops some of these ideas further when he talks about "strategic myopia"3. The directors/leaders of an organisation deliberately limit their range and scope of vision because it takes them too far from their "comfort zone".

Why is all this relevant in looking at Intrapreneurs?

The intrapreneur can break the cycle of decline. Even when the organisation is progressive and forward looking the intrapreneur can create additional drive and resourcefulness.

The idea that intrapreneurial activity in any organisation is driven from the top is quite fanciful. The driver for intrapreneurial activity is at the individual and interest group levels (see model above). The role of senior managers is to encourage individuals and interest groups and stand aside to let them work on their ideas as discussed by Daniel Pink in his book Drive[4]. This can be easier said than done. Here are some ideas on possible ways forward:

Creating the culture that encourages the Intrapreneur

Many organisations have developed very tight control systems with highly prescriptive systems and processes. This can be very positive but it can also limit the scope for the Intrapreneur. If staff have to account for every hour of their work with timesheets and similar reporting systems then it doesn't create the right environment if managers are focused on maximising the efficiency of running existing processes.

This top down approach to management and control can stifle the intrapreneur and even drive the people with the ideas out of the business – either to a competitor or to start their own business as an entrepreneur.

I propose a more balanced approach where the confidence that flows from having effective and realistic control systems enables greater empowerment and even autonomy throughout the organisation. There is also risk that informal silos will be created but this can be overcome if the organisation recognises the value of knowledge and how it can be managed effectively.

The information held within the formal control systems is just that – it is data and information. It is not knowledge. Knowledge is created by the way that individuals (at all levels) and groups of people apply the information and data to create improvements. For this to be effective the information and data must be shared and disseminated throughout the organisation. This can be quite challenging and sometimes it is necessary to limit access to some of the commercially sensitive information. Some of these limitations can be overcome by applying a simple factor to the original data so that the actual numbers are camouflaged.

How can all this information and data be developed into knowledge and learning which can help to drive the intrapreneurial culture?

There are some useful models which help the process of Knowledge Management. This is quite a complex range of theory which extends beyond the scope of this book but here's a summary which may help your thinking.

We start with the well known principle that there are two main types of knowledge – explicit and tacit.

Explicit knowledge is the documented and codified information which is structured in systems and processes to make it meaningful and useful to people doing their work. Examples will include the on-screen prompts used in call centres which is based on the accumulated experience of dealing with customer enquiries, complaints etc. Training manuals, quotation and tendering procedures along with the associated costing systems are also examples.

Tacit knowledge is what's in people's heads. It's difficult to codify because it is linked to the way the individual thinks and their experiences in dealing with certain situations. Tacit knowledge helps us to understand why different people can take the same information and interpret it in different ways. If used creatively these different thinking processes can drive innovations – and are key to building the intrapreneurial culture.

If we can keep capturing elements of tacit knowledge we can keep developing the explicit knowledge that can help us cope with "The Edge of Chaos" as described by Pascale earlier in the chapter.

A well documented approach to this progressive process was developed by Nonaka and Takeuchi with the SECI model[5]:

They start by defining knowledge management as "the capability of the organisation as a whole to create new knowledge, disseminate it throughout the organisation and quickly embody it in key products, services and systems".

This is where the intrapreneur can be a critical catalyst in revitalising an organisation and keeping it at the forefront of the industry/market.

They then put forward the process for achieving this knowledge management capability:

The key aim is to make the tacit knowledge explicit and available to others with the fours steps

Socialisation

Encouraging individuals and teams to share their tacit experiences and mental models through observation, imitation and discussion.

Externalisation

Articulation of the tacit knowledge through discourse and discussion on an iterative basis. Each iteration helps to clarify understanding and to develop understanding.

Combination

Combine the new ideas that develop from the externalisation stage with existing explicit knowledge to create a new level of knowledge.

Internalisation

With the new explicit knowledge base each individual and group can apply their own tacit knowledge to create a new platform for repeating the cycle.

This raises the important issue of how to create this dynamic learning environment. One way is to encourage the use of Communities of Practice[6]. This simply extends the use of both formal and informal groups but with a shared or common interest.

"Communities of practice are groups of people who share a concern, a set of problems, or a passion about a topic, and who deepen their knowledge and expertise in this area by interacting on an ongoing basis."

Source: Wenger et al, 2002[6]

"... shared experience within an CoP generates a 'shared repertoire' of communal resources that can be used as tools for enabling future practice. Arguably such tools could be divided into an information dimension ... and a tacit dimension. ... In close-knit CoPs, the tacit dimension can become highly aligned as practitioners ... share a similar way of interpreting and responding to information signals. .. (thus) emotional factors might be far more important than rational argument."

Source: Wenger, 2003[6]

These interpretations fit very closely with the way that entrepreneurs function and are therefore critical to understanding the way intrapreneurs need to be treated and nurtured.

CoPs provide a platform for building high performing teams – but they still require the support and encouragement of senior managers to give them the space, the autonomy and the freedom to act. It is critical to allow these CoPs and teams to experiment and make mistakes. This is the foundation of effective learning.

Soichiro Honda (the founder of Honda) is famous for the following statement:

"Many people dream of success. To me success can only be achieved through repeated failure and introspection. In fact success represents 1% in your work which results from the 99 percent that is called failure."

Check out his story from a young guy in pre-war Japan trying to sell piston rings to Toyota – there are lots of articles on the internet, just Google his name.

Teams must be encouraged to highlight and share their mistakes – other groups may have come up with solutions. Concealing mistakes loses the learning opportunity across the organisation.

So you've helped create some great teams producing exciting ideas. While many may be extensions of the existing product/service range some may go outside the current "comfort zone" of the organisation. How are all these ideas evaluated? It is this stage of the process that really tests the commitment of senior managers to the whole process of being open to new ideas and supporting the intrapreneurial culture.

Part of the problem goes back to the earlier comments in this chapter about entrenched views and attitudes about what the organisation "does". It is valid to consider the core strengths or competencies of the organisation but the real challenge is not to create core rigidities as suggested by

'the way we do things around here' may be an ingredient in current success but can lead to blinkered vision. 'Core competencies' are often linked with 'core rigidities' (Leonard-Barton)[7].

This is also underpinned by the work of Clayton Christensen on Disruptive Innovation[8] who suggests that large organisations tend to have a culture of their own and are very good at what they do but keep repeating the same processes and ideas for innovation and are vulnerable to radical change. Ideas that are generated should fit with the model of previous success or they risk being ignored, misunderstood or stifled by a system and senior managers that struggle to get out of their comfort zone.

Chris Argyris produced some great work on how organisations (or the people within them) control and learn[9]. He developed the basic single loop learning process into double loop learning discussed earlier in the book.

Single-loop learning involves knowing how to implement a particular process which is clearly defined from internal experience. A plan is established and implemented and the results monitored against the plan.

Double-loop learning goes much further and considering all the "governing variables" associated with the plan or project. This involves understanding the reasons for that process, questioning these assumptions, considers changes in the external environment that may have changed the whole rationale for the original project, learning from mistakes and considering ways in which they might be improved.

Argyris (1994) argued that one of the reasons organisations don't learn is that they are caught up in recurring defensive routines that prevent the openness required for double-loop learning.

Most organisations have a standardised way of presenting and evaluating projects – often linked to the single loop learning process. There will be the usual requirements for any project, typically:

Definition of the problem or opportunity

An outline of the proposed solution

An assessment of the resource and capability implications for the organization

Financial implications such as

Sales forecast

Costing structure showing key ratios such as Gross Profit %

Capital costs

Utilisation of existing resources

Forecasts for Profit/Loss, Balance Sheet and Cash Flow

Evaluation tools such as Discounted Cash Flow and Internal Rate of Return models

The problem is that while these are relevant and important they are often bench marked against the expectations for the existing organization. This might be a good starting point but it misses the opportunity to explore new opportunities and incorporate double loop learning. Adding this perspective could lead to further frameworks for evaluation such as:

An independent assessment of the external environment which focuses on future trends rather than the historical and current situation. Check out Chapter 8 on Strategy.

Assessment of the time scale for the introduction of new products/services particularly considering the expected life of current products/services and the Diffusion of Innovation Model proposed by Everett Rogers[10] which highlights how most new products and services build market penetration:

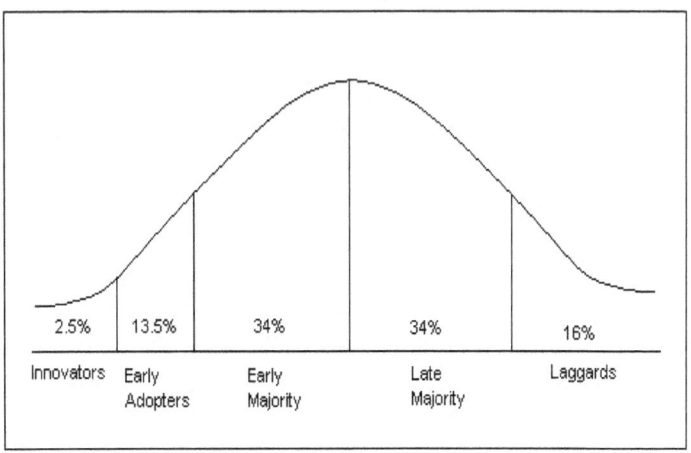

The insights from analysing the adoption process helps to guide the market research needed to fully evaluate the innovation. It is likely that the existing internal marketing processes will be focused on the existing product/service range and may not have the scope or expertise to effectively evaluate the market opportunities for an innovative product/service.

Competitor and supplier reaction will need to be evaluated as the innovative product/service may go beyond the scope of the "known" customers and suppliers.

The scope for new partnerships, joint ventures and collaborations should be investigated. This can be particularly important if the innovation goes into new markets or industries where the organization has limited experience.

All of this means that the established parameters for assessing projects may need to be re-evaluated such as targets for Internal Rate of Return[11].

Assessment of the business structure

Is the organization going to function as a Corporate Parent rather than manage the detail of the project?

How is funding to be organized?

Will the Corporate Parent act as a Venture Capitalist?

This raises issues of equity participation with the intrapreneurs and the role of the organization as a shareholder,

What are the reporting processes and contingency plans?

There is a common theme appearing here which helps to underpin the way a successful intrapreneur culture might be developed.

Support and full commitment from senior managers is critical – not just speeches and gestures.

The ability to be flexible and adaptive at all levels linked to the importance of empowerment and autonomy within the teams.

Willingness to recognise and work with the limitations of the existing organisation.

Promotion of a culture of genuine innovation, learning and risk taking linked to the acceptance of mistakes as a valuable platform for learning.

Keeping a critical and open mind linked to the ability to reflect on our own limitations and a willingness to celebrate diversity throughout the organisation at all levels.

This Chapter has tried to link a range of practical implications with some relevant theory. As in previous chapters the use of theory is limited to what is relevant for the level of understanding for this book. There are many more theories which might be applied and the changing-odds.com website is a platform for exploring some of these ideas – in a practical way.

Use the following blank page to review your answer to the introductory question and reflect on your learning from this chapter.

Chapter 14 - Distilling the Process

Now you've got to the end of the book you might be thinking that this all sounds great but how do I go about starting the business?

There's certainly a lot to take in and there are no perfect structures. As I've tried to emphasise throughout, every business start-up is different and from the very first idea to actually running a successful business requires flexibility, imagination, curiosity and the ability to change direction and respond to uncertainty. At the heart of the process is the need to manage a multitude of challenges – it is a management process. Oh yes – it also needs a lot of hard work.

This chapter aims to distil the overall content of the book into a sequence of actions that may help to structure your work in progressing from idea to successful business. Remember this is not a rigid process so be prepared to flex things but I hope the overall content provides you with a framework whether you are a sole trader with a lifestyle business or an aspiring unicorn – and everyone in between.

Before we start let me highlight an issue that worries many entrepreneurs – at what stage do we write the business plan? What should be included?

My answer is always the same – don't!

Why? Read this chapter and the answer appears at the end.

Starting Point – The Idea
This will come from a range of sources:

Curiosity

Why are things the way they are?

What could change?

What are the consequences and impact of these changes?

Not just for my own situation but customers, consumers, suppliers, the environment

Why am I doing this?

This should not be for profit. As Sinek[1] says profit is a result which simply flows from having a successful idea which satisfies customer needs and demands.

At this stage your head is full of ideas and it's often difficult to sort out all the potential opportunities. There are too many ideas and the challenge is just where to start. This is when it's important to get the ideas out of the head and onto some form of media where you can stand back and assess all the opportunities. There are many ways to do this – mind maps, post-it notes etc. Check out Chapter 3 for some possible approaches.

Stage 2 – Defining the Scope

Organising the ideas into priorities requires some initial research. Don't just rely on what you know – or think you know. Your view may be limited and there may even be "strategic myopia" as described in Chapter 8[2].

At this early stage you're defining the scope of the business. This may not be the finished article but provides you with a starting point from which you can build. This does not mean you don't have and retain the bigger, long term vision but you are starting to create a realistic structure based on building a profile of:

Customers and their "persona"

The Markets that you will compete in

The Industry that you will operate in

The Competition you will face
The Suppliers you will need
The Partners that may help you
This is the first level of strategic analysis as described in Chapter 8.

Stage 3 – Test the viability

This is the first cycle of a process that you will go through several times. You will assemble all the available information and start to formulate a plan around costing and pricing, customer expectations, the resources you will need.

Chapter 5 gives you a range of tools to check out if the business is capable of generating a profit and the potential scale of the business.

Stage 4 – Reflect and Refine

You have now developed an outline profile of the business and the potential scope and scale.

Now is a good opportunity to stand back and look at the evidence that you are compiling and reflect on the results.

Does the original idea still make sense?

Have you missed some opportunities?

Are there some threats that you have identified?

Is there scope to redefine some of the elements and improve the plan?

You might even have a trial to test your ideas as suggested by Eric Reis (The Lean Startup) and discussed in Chapter 1. As Reis suggests this may be a time to "pivot" or even walk away and start again. This should not be viewed as negative. It would be very negative to pursue an idea that isn't viable. This is an opportunity to learn and rethink – as discussed in Chapter 11.

Stage 5 – Confirm, adapt, pivot

You are now starting to firm up your ideas and actions. You should have a clear picture of your customers, their persona, their profile and their needs.

Now you need to define the resources and capabilities that are needed to meet these customer needs – and exceed them. This is covered in Chapter 8.

You should be considering the Minimum Viable Product[3] (MVP) and getting some details on:

Detailed costings
Pricing structures
Supply issues
Location of suppliers
Minimum order quantities
Supply lead times
Quality control and specification
Structure of the business
Partner relationships
Outline Terms and Conditions
Availability of suitable staff resources

Options for outsourcing – this may be necessary if early demand exceeds your capacity (Chapter 5)

With the MVP you might consider some rapid prototyping, beta testing and other ways to test the suitability of your product/service.

Stage 6 – Second stage viability test

You now have lots of detail so it's a good time to test the viability again. The same process as before but in more detail. It's at this stage that cash flow starts to become an important factor as this will impact on the level of funding needed and the time frames for the funding – see Chapter 6

You should also be assessing the likely impact of competitors and collaboration with partners. This is an important element in risk assessment. This is always a key area of interest from potential investors. If you are not clear on the issues with evidence to back up your claims then investors are likely to walk away – even from a great technological break through. Why? Because failure to adequately assess the risks and threats reflects a naïve and even arrogant approach which is not good for investor confidence.

Stage 7 – Refine, reflect, rethink – again.

At every stage of building and evaluating your idea you should take the time to review. Discuss the issues with others. This can be a great way to utilise the skills of a mentor.

You are building confidence and credibility. This stage may not take long. It may just be sleeping on it, but it's an important part of the learning process that is turning you into an expert in running a successful business. You might go back to the ideas in Chapter 13 and the ideas of Richard Pascale about "Surfing the edge of chaos" which highlights the importance of dealing with uncertainty and the dangers of "stability".

Stage 8 – Final Review (perhaps)

At this final stage you are pulling together all the strands of your idea and the practical implications for the business.

You will have clear picture of:

The product/service definition and scope

Why it is relevant and how it meets your customer needs and expectations

A definition of the customer persona

The scope of the business

The structure with systems and processes

Geographic scope

Confirmation of the business model
Terms and conditions for trade
The resources and capabilities within the business
Final costing and pricing framework
Assessment of the risks and sensitivities including seasonal trends, industry cycles and economic cycles
Financial forecasts driven by all the elements above and not just simple extrapolation
Profit and loss
Balance sheet
Cash flow
Funding requirements and sources

You have compiled a story that paints a realistic and evidence based picture of a future scenario. You have gone through stages of reflection, re-evaluation and even pivoting which demonstrates a critical and curious mindset and, importantly, the skills to learn and evolve your ideas in an uncertain world.

Quite simply – You now have a Business Plan that will stand up to any level of scrutiny.

Appendix 1

Common Formats

The UK has one of the easiest and most flexible structures for setting up and running any business. The flexibility is an important feature as it enables a progression from a simple structure to a more complex one as the business grows and develops. However, this does not limit starting with a more complex structure if this suits the needs of the business.

I will use this structure to illustrate the common features and characteristics of the various corporate forms.

Sole Trader

This is often linked to self-employment and is the simplest form and provides the opportunity for an individual to carry on a trade or profession while accepting all the risks and liabilities of the business on a personal basis. It's usually very simple and quick to set up – in the UK the individual just needs to notify the tax authorities within 3 months of starting to ensure that personal tax is covered through a self-assessment process requiring an annual tax return along with payment of any taxes due.

There is no corporation tax involved although the sole trader may need to register for Value Added Tax (VAT) subject to certain conditions on turnover etc.

In the UK there is a steady move towards all tax filings, payments, refunds etc to be handled on line and increasingly linked to electronic accounts systems. This is becoming quite straight forward with the availability of low cost (and sometimes free) online bookkeeping and accounting systems which take away much of the pain and problems of old fashioned, manual bookkeeping. Many of these system can be linked to the business bank account with many offerings provided by the so called "challenger" banks that provide reliable alternative banking facilities to the traditional banks.

It's important to take out appropriate insurance for any risks. This does not need to be expensive but the costs will depend on the type of business and the perceived risks.

For example, a self-employed plumber will be working at customer premises installing pipes, boilers etc. What happens if there is an accident or there is a fault in the building outside the control of the plumber – but there is major damage. This is where insurance comes in. Indeed, most customers won't use a tradesman unless they can demonstrate suitable insurance cover. Would you want someone in your house that might blow it up – and not have the resources to put it right?

Hairdressers may cut a client. A financial consultant may give the wrong advice. A chef may poison someone. Whatever you do insurance is a vital component – which applies to all types of business.

The big advantage of Sole Trader is the simplicity and privacy. You don't need to disclose anything except an annual tax return which is a private document between you and HMRC. You own everything but you are also personally liable for all debts and liabilities of the business.

Partnerships

At its simplest a partnership is a group of sole traders who have agreed to collaborate usually to provide a wider range of services or just greater capacity and scale.

Like a sole trader each partner takes responsibility for their individual tax situation and the self assessment tax returns will require a partnership return as well as the individual tax assessment.

It is important to have a partnership agreement signed by all partners. This should specify the agreed responsibilities for each partner. It is possible to have a "sleeping partner" who might just be providing finance under defined conditions. Having an agreement helps to handle the breakdown of the partnership – hopefully in an orderly and friendly way.

This leads us to an important feature of UK (and other regimes) partnership rules. Liabilities and responsibilities are "joint and several". In practice this means that each partner is jointly accountable and responsible for the liabilities of the partnership – except where exclusions are specified in a formal partnership agreement.

Each partner can be pursued by a bank for the repayment of a loan. While it is normal to pursue all the partners an individual partner may be pursued for the full amount. This may be an issue for the remaining partners if one of the partners becomes difficult to locate, becomes bankrupt etc.

So be very careful both in picking your partners and also ensure there is a formal legal partnership agreement that confirms any variations in responsibility, for example, provisions for a "sleeping partner". The agreement should also cover the process of ending the partnership. If just one partner leaves the partnership this effectively ends the whole partnership agreement because the relationship between the remaining partners has changed. The partnership agreement should be re-written to reflect this even if the main structure and substance of the agreement stay the same.

If the partners agree to wind up the partnership (cease operation) then the partnership agreement will cover the process of how this will be done. This is particularly important to avoid disputes about the distribution of any profits and assets within the partnership – and the allocation of responsibilities for dealing with liabilities.

Limited Liability

The focus in this section will be on the UK model (this is what I know). Different countries have different legal and taxation structures so if you're not based in the UK then you will need to check the local requirements.

It's not my intention to go into the technical and legal aspects of taxation etc – this is a specialised field which I'm not qualified to talk about. What I provide here is a general "practitioner" approach to understanding the features, benefits and drawbacks of the most common forms of business structure. The important issue is to design your business structure to meet your purpose and your long-term goals.

Limited liability in it's current form has been around in most countries for over 150 years. It was introduced in the UK during the mid 19th century to encourage wealthy landowners and merchants to invest part of their wealth and assets in the new developments of the industrial revolution – in particular the railway network. This was developed using private capital and was seen by some as highly risky – a bit like the internet when it started.

Prior to limited liability everyone was treated as an individual and was responsible for their own debts. If you got things wrong you could end up in debtors prison. The limited liability principles are enshrined in a progression of acts of Parliament – the Companies Act – which is updated every so often (usually around every 20 years or so).

The legislation creates a separate legal 'personality' for the company which means that investors are only exposed to the risk of losing their investment if the business fails – rather than potentially unlimited liability of trading as an individual. This investor protection is provided in return for disclosure and transparency of the relevant commercial and financial information by the shareholders and investors.

The shareholders are entitled to be paid dividends from the profits of the business. There are quite specific rules for the way dividends can be calculated and paid. These may vary depending on the "class of share". Shares can be issued with specific rules and shareholder rights around voting at General Meetings, levels of dividend etc. The details go beyond the scope of this book.

This disclosure process starts with the registration of the company at Companies House (or equivalent). The registration shows the original shareholders, the share structure, the directors and also sets out the objectives and constitution (how the business is managed in overall terms) of the company in the form of Memorandum and Articles of Association. All of this is in the public domain.

Each year the company has to update the shareholder information along with any changes to the shareholding structure – this is the Confirmation Statement. In addition the company must file annual accounts which are also published.

In the UK the accounts submitted for publication with Companies House can be very brief if the company is small. As the company gets larger (turnover etc) then the detail of disclosure increases.

As the company grows it has the option (but not an obligation) to move from a Private Limited Company to a Public Limited Company (PLC). This adds to the requirements on disclosure and there is a minimum capital requirement for the company – currently £50,000 for a UK company. Check out the details for your own country.

Once a company becomes a PLC it has the option of selling shares on a stock market – there are a number of these around the world. There is a common misconception about the status of the PLC in the UK. There is no requirement to list (trade) a company's shares on a stock market – this is simply a method of raising new capital by broadening the investor base. When a company decides to float (a common term for listing) on a stock market there is no requirement to float all the shares and it is quite common to only float as many as are needed to fund the next stages of growth.

Currently only about 10% of PLCs in the UK are listed on a stock market.

In the UK the whole process of setting up and running a business is very flexible and there are very few rigid rules about how you can set the business up.

As an example

Some years ago I was running a workshop for company directors about their responsibilities and how to run an effective board. The introductions went round the room with the usual range of people from Small and Medium Enterprise (SMEs) to a director of a large listed company. The exception was a person who explained he was a sole trader. This raised some eyebrows and a few looks of disdain. The curiosity became interesting when he acknowledged he wasn't a director (so why was he there?) but he was looking at converting to a limited company and needed to decide whether to start with a private limited company or jump straight to Public Limited Company (plc). More bemused looks from the other delegates. He then explained that as a sole trader he was currently turning over £2 million per year, making a substantial profit and employed around 50 staff with full office facilities.

All of this growth had been self-funded organic growth over about 10 years with only minimal support from the banks.

He converted to a limited company (not plc) and continued to grow and expand.

The Limited Company structure is also useful when the founder wants to sell the business or retire and enjoy the fruits of all the labour. As the company can last in perpetuity and has a requirement to appoint managers (directors) it is a much easier process to sell the shares or the assets which are clearly defined within the company structure.

All of these types of company are limited by shares as the way of measuring the liability of the shareholders.

There is also the option to set up a limited liability company where the liability is a guarantee. This is a structure primarily aimed at charities and social enterprises where profits may not be the primary objective. A Company Limited by Guarantee does not have shareholders – because there are no shares. Instead it has Members who each provide a guarantee to contribute a sum of money to contribute to any shortfall in the event that the company fails or closes. This is usually a nominal amount, often only £10 or £20.

Because there are no shareholders the company can't pay dividends – all profits must be recycled and invested back into the business. This highlights why this structure is common for charities and social enterprises.

This raises an interesting point about definitions. Charities and social enterprises are often described as Not for Profit (NFP) organisations. I find this a misleading definition as I have come across directors of these companies who really believe they are not allowed to make profits. This is just not true. Indeed, if the company doesn't make profits (or surpluses) then it won't be able to build up reserves. These reserves help the organisation plan and invest in future activities and provide a buffer if a stream of funding (donations or grants) is disrupted. Such disruption can be quite common. Without surpluses and reserves the organisation can quickly become insolvent and the directors have a responsibility to close it down if there is no prospect of trading through the crisis.

There are two relatively recent additions to the corporate structure scene:

Limited Liability Partnerships

These are effectively a hybrid between a Partnership and a limited liability company. This is often used by professional firms such as accountants, architects and solicitors but can be used for most types of business. The same general principle applies – the partners liability can be limited in return for disclosure of relevant financial and commercial information to the public domain.

Community Interest Companies (CIC)

These are designed to allow social enterprises to use a structure which enables shareholders to be rewarded with dividends albeit at a limited scale. This is intended to encourage investment by "social entrepreneurs" who want to invest for social projects but expect some degree of financial return.

A CIC must first be set up as a company through Companies House – either limited by shares or guarantee. It must apply to become a CIC through the CIC Regulator and comply with some quite stringent rules on payment of dividends and the disposal of assets (an asset lock).

Details on UK rules can be found through the following links but check out your own local rules and guidelines[1]:
https://www.gov.uk/set-up-sole-trader
https://www.gov.uk/set-up-business-partnership

https://www.gov.uk/guidance/set-up-and-run-a-limited-liability-partnership-llp
https://www.gov.uk/limited-company-formation
https://www.gov.uk/government/organisations/office-of-the-regulator-of-community-interest-companies

https://www.gov.uk/set-up-a-social-enterprise?step-by-step-nav=37e4c035-b25c-4289-b85c-c6d36d11a763

All of this knowledge is not just useful when you set up a business but is invaluable when you start trading. When you go looking for customers, suppliers, partners etc you should check out their legal status. If they're a limited company you can check them out at Companies House or the equivalent where you are located. If they're small the filed accounts may be very limited but there are always clues. At the minimum there will be a short balance sheet – what does the "equity" look like? If it's going up then it can suggest profits which are being retained. Who are the directors and do they have other interests with other businesses?

You might be able to spot a possible scam. A start up I was helping in the building sector rang me very excitedly to say he'd been approached by a property maintenance company wanting to sub-contract large amounts of work. I got the details and discovered:

There was a limited company registered at Companies House with a single director (quite legal).

However, the contract business was not trading under the limited company but T/A (trading as) a similar name but not actually using the Ltd tag.

It then emerged that the father of the sole director was a disqualified company director – information available from Companies House.

All of this raised issues about which legal entity would be contracting the work. A common scam in the building industry (and others) is to commission lots of small sub-contractors, get them to do lots of work perhaps with a small initial payment and then leave them chasing payment. I've known this trick to run for months with a long list of excuses for not paying. Either the company just disappears or they make it very difficult for the small sub-contractor to pursue the money.

This is not limited to small companies. Some years ago a major quoted construction group allegedly used the same techniques to delay/avoid payment. They set up an office to exclusively handle legal claims from sub-contractors and suppliers using every technique to avoid payment.

This is where understanding the law around non-payment is useful. Look up Statutory Demand to see how it works in the UK. Many small business owners don't know about this simple mechanism.

In the case of the major construction company mentioned above, there seemed to be a simple formula. Delay as much as possible and when a Statutory Demand arrives, check it and pay it to avoid the possibility of being declared bankrupt[2].

https://www.gov.uk/statutory-demands/forms-to-issue-a-statutory-demand

I was approached by a self-employed consultant retained to advise the same company on a range of technical building issues. The senior manager of the construction company had known the consultant for many years and it seemed like a good earning opportunity. The first tranche of work was completed and paid for. The work then continued – but no payments despite regular monthly invoices. The senior manager was now not contactable (no surprise there). I was asked what he should do. When told the name of the client company I explained about their reputation. He went white – he was owed around £80,000.

He weighed the risks of losing future work with the (still) large construction group against the current debt and the risk of not being paid in the future. The thought process didn't take long. He downloaded the documentation from the internet and submitted a Statutory Demand. He received full payment in 7 days.

The moral of the story – size matters but it doesn't guarantee anything and there are some very unpleasant people running businesses of all size so be cautious and suspicious.

Notes for each chapter

Chapter 1

1. Eric Ries, The Lean Startup, Penguin Books. Page 3

Chapter 2

1. https://www.gov.uk/set-up-sole-trader

    https://www.gov.uk/set-up-business-partnership
    https://www.gov.uk/guidance/set-up-and-run-a-limited-liability-partnership-llp
    https://www.gov.uk/limited-company-formation
    https://www.gov.uk/government/organisations/office-of-the-regulator-of-community-interest-companies
    https://www.gov.uk/set-up-a-social-enterprise?step-by-step-nav=37e4c035-b25c-4289-b85c-c6d36d11a763

2. https://www.gov.uk/statutory-demands/forms-to-issue-a-statutory-demand

Chapter 3

1. https://www.ted.com/talks/simon_sinek_how_great_leaders_inspire_action?language=en

The video highlights some key features about the way we should think about the business idea. There are some important issues linked to other parts of the book such as the Innovation Adopter Curve.

2. Webvan Case Study:
   https://groundfloorpartners.com/lessons-from-webvan/

Just one of many case studies analysing the rise and fall of this unicorn.

3. https://www.peapod.com/
4. https://www.tesco.com/
5. Amazon.com – 2002. S Leschly, M J Roberts, W A Sahlman Harvard Business Review Rev Feb 2003 (9-803-908)
6. Harry Potter – a series of books which transformed fictional reading particularly among young readers. Created by JK Rowlings.

Chapter 4

1. Jonathan A Knee, The Platform Delusion – who wins and who loses in the age of tech titans, 2021, Penguin Random House LLC.
2. https://www.nytimes.com/2005/07/28/technology/reading-between-the-lines-of-used-book-sales.html
3. https://www.inditex.com/
4. https://www.hm.com/entrance.ahtml?orguri=%2F
5. www.primark.com

6. Economist.com/business/2021/08/21/how-primark-makes-money-selling-350-t-shirts

7. Against the Grain: How I Went from Factory Floor to My Own Multi-Million Pound Company (and you could too) Graham Harris, 2018.

8. Yale Tribune 18May 2018 by JL2977

9. http://www.innospace.co.uk/about/events/business-start-boot-camp

Innospace is an incubator for start-ups and early stage businesses and runs regular bootcamps and workshops to support entrepreneurs.

10. Naomi Timperley –

11. https://globalnews.ca/news/7835722/peloton-recall-treadmill-child-death/#:~:text=Peloton%20and%20U.S.%20regulators%20have,over%20the%20last%20few%20years.&text=%E2%80%9CA%206%2Dyear%2Dold,treadmill%2C%E2%80%9D%20the%20CPSC%20said.

12. https://www.investopedia.com/terms/p/priceelasticity.asp

13. https://news.airbnb.com/airbnb-fourth-quarter-and-full-year-2020-financial-results/

https://www.airbnb.com/

14. Rogers, Everett (16 August 2003). Diffusion of Innovations, 5th Edition. Simon and Schuster. ISBN 978-0-7432-5823-4
15. "crossing the chasm" to get mainstream approval/acceptance of your product or service.

https://www.ted.com/talks/simon_sinek_how_great_leaders_inspire_action/transcript?language=en

16. Eric Ries, The Lean Startup, Penguin Books p99 and beyond.
17. Daniel Pink – To sell is human. A great book on the realities and myths around selling.

Chapter 5

1. Richard Rumelt, Good Strategy/Bad Strategy
2. https://www.airbnb.com/

www.uber.com
www.deliveroo.com

3. Eric Reis, the Lean Startup. Minimum Viable Product pp104-5 plus lots of other examples.

Chapter 6

1. Mark R Tercek and Jonathan S Adams, Nature's Fortune, Basic Books, 2013.
2. http://www.innospace.co.uk/about/events/business-start-boot-camp

Innospace is an incubator for start-ups and early stage businesses and runs regular bootcamps and workshops to support entrepreneurs.

3. https://esmeefairbairn.org.uk/
4. https://www.johnmuirtrust.org/
5. https://businessfightspoverty.org/

Chapter 7

1. David Guest "The hunt is on for the Renaissance Man of computing," in The Independent, September 17, 1991.
2. McKinsey & Company as presented - Johnston, D. L. (1978). Scientists Become Managers-The "T"-Shaped Man. IEEE Engineering Management Review, 6(3), 67–68. doi:10.1109/emr.1978.4306682

3. Richard Rumelt, Good Strategy, Bad Strategy, 2011, Profile Books Ltd
4. David Robson, The Intelligence Trap, 2019, Hodder and Stoughton.

Chapter 8

1. Richard Rumelt, Good Strategy, Bad Strategy, 2011, Profile Books Ltd
2. Richard Rumelt, Good Strategy, Bad Strategy, 2011, Profile Books Ltd, p77
3. Richard Rumelt, Good Strategy, Bad Strategy, 2011, Citation of John Mamer, p79
4. Simon Sinek – Start with Why.

https://www.ted.com/talks/simon_sinek_how_great_leaders_inspire_action?language=en

5. Fahey, L., & Narayanan, V. K.
   (1986). Macroenvironmental Analysis for Strategic Management (The West Series in Strategic Management). St. Paul, Minnesota: West Publishing Company.
6. Michael E Porter, How Competitive Forces shape Strategy, 1979 Harvard Business Review. This has been updated several times but the core of the thinking remains the same.
7. Richard Rumelt, Good Strategy, Bad Strategy, 2011, Profile Books Ltd, pp 280-281.

8. Barney, J. B. (1991). Firm resources and sustained competitive advantage. Journal of Management, 17, 99–120.
9. Grant, Robert M., (1991) "The resource-based theory of competitive advantage: implications for strategy formulation" from California Management Review 33 (3) pp.114-135, Berkeley, Calif.: University of California ©
10. Mind Genius.com

Chapter 9

Chapter 10

1. Superforecasting: The Art and Science of Prediction is a book by Philip E. Tetlock and Dan Gardner released in 2015. It details findings from The Good Judgment Project.
2. John Kay and Mervyn King, Radical Uncertainty, https://www.youtube.com/watch?v=Rc73PCAN1Vg
3. Intergovernmental Panel on Climate Change AR6 https://www.ipcc.ch/report/ar6/wg1/
4. John Kay, Obliquity, 2010. Obliquity: Why our goals are best achieved indirectly is a book by economist John Kay. It was inspired by an observation of the successful pharmaceutical researcher, Sir James Black: I used to tell my colleagues that if they wanted to make money, there were many easier ways to do it than drug research.

Chapter 11

1. Joseph Schumpeter was an Austrian economist who is famous for his interpretation of capitalism: According to Schumpeter, the "gale of creative destruction" describes the "process of industrial mutation that continuously revolutionizes the economic structure from within, incessantly destroying the old one, incessantly creating a new one". This is often used to support the argument of not supporting businesses or even industries that have outlived their usefulness.
2. Chris Argyris Chris Argyris, On Organizational Learning, 1992, Blackwell Publishers, Massachusetts, USA
3. Double loop Learning, Chris Argyris
4. Intrapeneurs – those working within an organization who may help to change the direction of the organization and even disrupt the existing one. Entrepreneurial thinking but within an existing organization.
5. Edgar Schein, The levels of culture, Organizational Culture and Leadership. 2004. Jossey-Bass
6. Taken from Argyris, Putnam & McLain Smith (1985, p. 89)
7. Argyris and Schön 1996; Bolman and Deal 1997: 147-8)
8. Extracted from Smith, M. K. (2001, 2013). 'Chris Argyris: theories of action, double-loop learning and organizational learning', the encyclopedia of informal education. [http://infed.org/mobi/chris-argyris-theories-of-action-double-loop-learning-and-organizational-learning/.

There are some great links to a range of work from great idea generators and this article gives some good insights into the practical application of the ideas.

9. Chris Argyris, On Organizational Learning, 1992, Blackwell Publishers, Massachusetts, USA
10. Chris Argyris, Teaching smart people how to learn, Harvard Business Review, 2004
11. Fahey, L., & Narayanan, V. K. (1986). Macroenvironmental Analysis for Strategic Management (The West Series in Strategic Management). St. Paul, Minnesota: West Publishing Company.

Chapter 12

1. Maslow A, "A Theory of Human Motivation" (originally published in Psychological Review, 1943, Vol. 50 #4, pp. 370–396).
2. Mobileye – the future of driverless cars, David Yoffie, Harvard Business School, October 28, 2015, 9-715-421.

3. Silver spoon is a term sometimes used to describe those from a wealthy and/or privileged background which has been created by a previous generation. It may not be a fair description of many who are in inherited privileged situations.

Chapter 13

1. PASCALE, R. T. (1999) 'SURFING THE EDGE OF CHAOS', SLOAN MANAGEMENT REVIEW, SPRING 1999, PP. 83–94. Treating organizations as complex adaptive systems provides powerful insights into the nature of strategic work.
2. Johnson, Scholes and Whittington, 2008, p. 180, Exploring Corporate Strategy, Pearson Books.
3. Richard Rumelt, Strategic myopia, Good Strategy, Bad Strategy, px
4. The thinking behind "standing aside" is put forward by Daniel Pink in Drive and in his video

https://www.youtube.com/watch?v=y1SDV8nxypE

5. Nonaka, I. and Takeuchi, H. (1995) The Knowledge-Creating Company: How Japanese Companies Create the Dynamics of Innovation, Oxford, Oxford University Press
6. Wenger, E. (2003) 'Communities of practice and social learning systems' in Nicolini, D., Gherardi, S. and Yanow, D. (eds) Knowing in Organizations: A Practice-Based Approach, New York, M. E. Sharpe. Wenger, E., McDermott, R. and Snyder, W. M. (2002) Cultivating Communities of Practice: A Guide to Managing Knowledge, Boston, MA, Harvard Business School Press.
7. Leonard-Barton, D. (1998) Wellsprings of Knowledge: Building and Sustaining the Sources of Innovation, Boston, MA, Harvard Business School Press
8. https://www.christenseninstitute.org/disruptive-innovations/

9. Chris Argyris, On Organizational Learning, 1992, Blackwell Publishers, Massachusetts, USA
10. Rogers, Everett M. (1983). Diffusion of innovations (3rd ed.). New York: Free Press of Glencoe. ISBN 9780029266502.

This is also highlighted in the Simon Sinek video – Why?

11. IRR stands for Internal Rate of Return which is a common way to assess the financial value of a long term project often lasting several years. It uses the concept of discounted cash flow which recognises that a unit of money today is worth more than a promised unit of money in the future. Other approaches for assessing projects include pay back period and net present value.

Chapter 14

1. Simon Sinek – Start with Why.

https://www.ted.com/talks/simon_sinek_how_great_leaders_inspire_action?language=en

2. Richard Rumelt, Strategic myopia, Good Strategy, Bad Strategy, p260.
3. Eric Reis, The Lean Startup, Minimum Viable Product used to test the acceptability of a new product or service.

Acknowledgements

In writing this book I've talked to and listened to some great people who are a mix of friends, professional colleagues, clients, students I've tutored – in fact as many people as I could find who would listen and contribute.

I can't acknowledge everyone but the following warrant special mention:

My colleague at Innospace and the manager is Louise Kenworthy who is both a great friend and a positive influence in developing many of the ideas and material which impacts on this book and is a driver for our workshops and bootcamps for entrepreneurs.
The team that deliver the workshops and bootcamps and provide mentoring support have a great influence:
Naomi Timperley – social media and marketing
Mike Braun – tax and accountancy
Durham Grigg – Intellectual property and legal
Paul Tucker – mentoring and project evaluation

There is a long list of great people who have provided informal advice, proof reading and critical feedback on the drafts:
Paul Mills – successful entrepreneur with many years' experience and an innovative thinker.
Dominik Rose – successful technology entrepreneur
Joe Tunstall – student with a great business idea who has provided insights into the younger entrepreneurs needs

John Evans – a colleague on MBA strategy tutoring programmes

Fabian Weingart – a wonderful sounding board who greatly influenced the chapters on the types of entrepreneurs and the challenges facing an intrapreneur.

Emma Beard and Victoria Maher for developing the book cover design, the website platform and the overall branding and copy.

Shai Schechter – some great stories and insights into technology start-ups.

Gerhard Seiler – a great technology innovator.

Paul Seligman – Chairman of Captivate Group who provided some great ideas around presentation and style.

For those that I've not included who believe a mention is deserved just drop me a note and I'll happily update the list.

Finally, every start-up that I've worked with deserves a mention. Please come to the website:

www.changing-odds.com – and tell your story.

I have tried to provide recognition and acknowledgement to sources of material used in the book. If I have missed anyone then this is an oversight for which I apologise. If you feel you deserve credit please let me know and I'll try to update the acknowledgements, notes and references in a future edition.

www.ingramcontent.com/pod-product-compliance
Lightning Source LLC
Chambersburg PA
CBHW072152100526
44589CB00015B/2195